Praise for *Customer Loyalty Guaranteed*

"Service excellence begins with leaders who are passionate about creating an extraordinary experience for customers by developing a supportive work environment for associates. *Customer Loyalty Guaranteed* is as inspirational as it is instructive."
—Horst Schulze, retired president, The Ritz-Carlton Hotel Company, and CEO, West Paces Hotels

"*Customer Loyalty Guaranteed* is one of the best books I have ever read on creating memorable experiences for your Guests and motivating and retaining the talent that creates the experience—your valued Associates, through true understanding of what makes all the critical players tick. This is one book we will share with all of our teams to help make the Build-A-Bear Workshop experience even better!"
—Maxine Clark, founder, Chief Executive Bear, Build-A-Bear Workshop

"Chip and John show leaders practical ways to inspire and develop the unique talents of their staff. In turn, they demonstrate how your employees can produce the type of experience that inspires your customers to be an extension of your sales force."
—Joseph A. Michelli, author, *The Starbucks Experience*

"*Customer Loyalty Guaranteed* will help transform your team at every level and your customers with each experience into advocates of your core culture. It's leadership built on trust every day."
—Rudy Borneo, vice chairman, Macy's West

"Customers are loyal to organizations passionate about creating excellence. Chip Bell and John Patterson provide a cutting-edge blueprint for excellence targeted for those who serve customers and those who serve associates."
—Roberto R. Herencia, president, Banco Popular North America

Praise for *Customer Loyalty Guaranteed*

"Chip and John have a unique understanding of what it takes to turn customers into devoted advocates for your company. *Customer Loyalty Guaranteed* gives you direct access to that knowledge and the tools to build a team that is focused on service, loyalty, and success."

—Larry Merlo, president, CVS/Pharmacy Retail

"Chip and John understand the distinction between just satisfying customers' needs and creating meaningful customer experiences. Their stories and insights provide the elements needed for creating positive emotional relationships that last."

—Dean Eisner, CEO, Manheim

"The goal of all great service organizations is to develop and retain those team players referred to as 'Loyalty Creators' in *Customer Loyalty Guaranteed* by Bell and Patterson. This book should become the playbook for any team wishing to achieve greatness as a service organization. Believe me, their formula works!!!!!"

—Ann Rhoads, cofounder and EVP of People, JetBlue Airways

"Loyal customers love organizations with a super fantastic service attitude! *Customer Loyalty Guaranteed* shows how to get it, how to use it, and how to keep it!"

—Keith Harrell, author, *Attitude Is Everything!*

"The authors give us a wonderful gift. They provide an exciting new model for developing loyal customers and simultaneously teach us the art and science of how leaders can keep their best employees engaged and retained."

—Beverly Kaye, author, *Love 'Em or Lose 'Em*

Praise for *Customer Loyalty Guaranteed*

"*Customer Loyalty Guaranteed* is required reading for anyone who comes face-to-face with customers plus anyone who supports or leads those who do. Buy it, read it, and apply it. You'll find it more than worth the investment . . . guaranteed."

—Jim Kouzes, author, *Leadership Challenge*

"Read this book, and put the ideas into action and you will do exactly as the title suggests, you'll guarantee customer loyalty. If you have customers, read this book."

—Kevin Eikenberry, author, *Remarkable Leadership*

"If you are anywhere near a customer, you need to read *Customer Loyalty Guaranteed* and then read it again! Loyal customers are not born, they are made, and this roadmap shows you exactly how to do it."

—Bill Rose, founder & executive director, Service & Support Professionals Association (SSPA)

"*Customer Loyalty Guaranteed* is the BEST book on customer loyalty I have ever read!"

—Paul Cardis, CEO, AVID Ratings

★ ★ ★ ★ ★

CUSTOMER LOYALTY
GUARANTEED

Create, Lead, and
Sustain Remarkable
Customer Service

CHIP R. BELL AND JOHN R. PATTERSON

Avon, Massachusetts

Interior illustrations by Mark DiVico.

Published by Adams Business, an imprint of Adams Media, an F + W Publications Company
57 Littlefield Street
Avon, MA 02322
www.adamsmedia.com

Printed in the United States of America.

J I H G F E D C B A

ISBN-10: 1-59869-468-5
ISBN-13: 978-1-59869-468-0

Library of Congress Cataloging-in-Publication Data
Bell, Chip R.
Customer loyalty guaranteed / Chip R. Bell and John R. Patterson.
 p.   cm.
Includes bibliographical references and index.
ISBN-13: 978-1-59869-468-0 (pbk.)
ISBN-10: 1-59869-468-5 (pbk.)
1. Customer relations. 2. Customer loyalty. 3. Customer services.
I. Patterson, John R. II. Title.
HF5415.5.B4337 2007
658.8'12—dc22   2007018991

This publication is designed to provide accurate and authoritative information with regard to the subject matter covered. It is sold with the understanding that the publisher is not engaged in rendering legal, accounting, or other professional advice. If legal advice or other expert assistance is required, the services of a competent professional person should be sought.
　—From a *Declaration of Principles* jointly adopted by a Committee of the American Bar Association and a Committee of Publishers and Associations

Many of the designations used by manufacturers and sellers to distinguish their product are claimed as trademarks. Where those designations appear in this book and Adams Media was aware of a trademark claim, the designations have been printed with initial capital letters.

This book is available at quantity discounts for bulk purchases.
For information, please call 1-800-289-0963.

To Nancy Rainey Bell
and
Katie Bunch Patterson

Contents

PART ONE

PART TWO

PART THREE

Acknowledgments

Book writing is never a solo activity. The archaic picture of an introverted author cloistered in a quiet room with writing instrument and maddening moments of mental silence is a complete myth. Many people gather around the author or authors to transform rough words on an uncaring computer screen into polished prose that becomes animated on a printed page.

This is our chance to express our gratitude to the many who gathered with us. Like those awkward moments on all award nights, we are likely to forget someone we should thank.

We begin our thank you's with our great clients, for the powerful lessons they have taught us about this topic. We are especially grateful to the senior leaders of Pegasus Solutions, Banco Popular, McDonald's Corporation, General Growth Properties, EDiS Corporation, Southern California Edison, Aurora HealthCare, Freeman, Kaiser Permanente, Marriott, Banco Continental, Duke Energy, Ritz-Carlton Hotel Company, Federated, Manheim, GlaxoSmithKline, and Lockheed Martin. We have also benefited from the thought-provoking questions and powerful insights delivered by many of the consulting partners of the Chip Bell Group.

Our world-class editor, Dave Zielinski, gave us his special brand of vernacular wisdom. He made the editing process easy, meeting every tight deadline imposed on him with his signature can-do style that gives authors confidence. This is Chip's third book with Dave—enough said! Our literary agent, Laurie Harper, found us Adams Media, a partnership that made the book production process extremely pleasurable. With Adams Media came our publishing editor, Jill Alexander, and our managing editor, Laura Daly, who shared our commitment to this book and our passion to make it successful. We have high expectations because of their special contributions.

Finally, this book would not have happened without the emotional sustenance and ingenious inspiration of our families and especially our life partners, Nancy Bell and Katie Patterson. They took up the slack many, many times to allow us the freedom to have late-night editorial discussions long past all our bedtimes.

To all of you: Thanks!

INTRODUCTION
The Case for Customer Loyalty

Customers are attracted to spirited people. Too often, what they encounter instead are workers offering indifferent, robotic, or rude service. Customers routinely see service employees sleepwalking through their workdays. They might also see other better-intentioned coworkers who are trapped in service systems designed for internal convenience but not customer delight. Customers long to interact with—even relate to—employees who act like there is still a light on inside.

Organizations have a new label for the kind of spirited, motivated employees that customers seek—engaged! No longer is the focus on employee longevity or the expectation that workers will salute the organizational flag. Today it's more about keeping people as passionate and productive as possible. Most organizations would much rather have a fired-up employee for the short term than an uninspired one who's simply collecting a paycheck over the long haul.

Organizations now have metrics that convincingly demonstrate the link between employee engagement and customer loyalty, as well as the all-important tie between customer loyalty and profitable growth. Happy employees make happy customers, and happy customers buy, advocate, forgive, and, most importantly, return. While there are plenty of resources on how to keep score on employee engagement, far fewer resources describe how to raise and sustain that score. Besides, metric mania can seduce leaders into focusing on the scoreboard while losing track of what's happening in the game.

No matter how comprehensive and accurate our modern metrics may be, they will never completely capture the magic and mystery of an engaged and spirited relationship. By focusing too heavily on objective data, tidy calculations, and sterilized reports, leaders are losing touch with the fact that they are putting precious energy on the *least* important reality concerning the customer, the employee, or the leader.

The life expectancy of the average company today is between forty and fifty years. For instance, of the companies listed as a 1980 *Fortune* 500 company, only 113 remained on the list for 2007. Yet some companies last for centuries. According to Arie De Geus, author of *The Living Company*, the most enduring have four things in common:

1. They find ways to keep passion and spirit in the culture.
2. They are sensitive to their environment.
3. They keep a strong sense of identity.
4. They tolerate employee eccentricities and activities on the margin.

In a phrase, they act like living, spirited organisms.

The Nature of Organizational Spirit

Enterprises are born with spirit—an energy or vision that connects them and their products and/or services to the customer. As companies grow, the need for standardization, efficiency, and enhanced productivity ushers in new processes, structures, and procedures. Initially, spirit and bureaucracy coexist. After a time, however, there is a battle between the intuitive, heart-driven visionary and the rational, brain-driven administrator. For many companies, process soundly defeats passion.

Yet to be effective, enterprises must find a way to balance efficiency with enthusiasm. If the rational side routinely trumps the emotional, it encourages employees to become robotic and rules-obsessed.

In insular organizations ruled by a steely-eyed rationality, customers are often viewed as a distraction. Leaders in these companies tend to believe that customers act in a random, illogical, and selfish fashion, too often failing to follow the company's carefully scripted procedures. In short, customers upset the tidiness of organizational order.

Yet customers are vital for any organization. As Wal-Mart founder Sam Walton once remarked, "There is only one boss. The customer. And he can fire everybody in the company from the chairman on down, simply by spending his money somewhere else."

One of the best ways of ensuring more of those precious dollars stay in-house is to implement systems and leadership practices that ensure your organization is dominated not by the dispassionate and detached, but by engaged and committed employees who burn with a fire for serving customers.

What Is This Book About?

Customer Loyalty Guaranteed is designed to help leaders make the employee-customer connection a force for competitive advantage. The more that employees give passion and spirit, the more customers will reward that organization with their loyalty.

The book doesn't just describe an organizational strategy; it outlines a way of life. People who adopt this philosophy tend to elevate all their relationships, nurturing them in a fashion that acknowledges them as special and valuable. It is more than the Golden Rule personified—it is a way to strike a better balance between heart and head in pursuit of business excellence. For believers in the philosophy, it is the reason they come to work each day.

Customer Loyalty Guaranteed is divided into three parts. Part One, "Meet the Loyalty Creators," profiles seven employees skilled at creating loyal customers. Each type demonstrates a different trait or ability essential to building an almost unbreakable bond between organization and customer. This section of the book is crafted to illustrate employee engagement in action and give readers a deeper understanding of its nature. Before leaders can create and nurture the passion to serve, they must recognize it when they see it and understand its component parts. Part Two, "Leading Your Loyalty Creators," focuses on how leaders nurture the service performance of Loyalty Creators. These

Loyalty Creators very often serve customers in the manner they are served by their leaders. Part Three, "Sustaining Remarkable Service," zeroes in on the vital elements needed to sustain remarkable service. The quality of service delivered consistently over time is a function of whether the work climate is customer-centric. This section provides tools and techniques for ensuring a service attitude is imbedded into the DNA of the organization.

Going Beyond "Satisfaction"

Take a drive down the main boulevard in any city and read the billboards. You'll see any number of marketing pitches featuring language like "Satisfaction guaranteed," "Your satisfaction is our number-one goal," or "We are #1 in customer satisfaction." You might assume that *satisfaction* was the ticket to high praise, robust profits, and repeat business. But unless your organization is the only fish in the pond, using customer satisfaction as a yardstick of success will ultimately lead to disappointment, maybe even failure.

As a growing amount of service quality research has found, measures of "satisfaction" are often poor predictors of the most important of all customer service goals: Will customers who visit you once keep coming back for more? Will they stay fervently loyal, producing the welcome byproducts of lower marketing or customer acquisition costs, fewer defections, more word-of-mouth recommendations, and ultimately stronger profits?

While the use of rating terms like "very satisfied" or "satisfied" on customer surveys might be sufficient to gauge customers' assessment of products, these descriptors often fall woefully short of predicting customer loyalty. This loyalty can be defined as a firm intention to repurchase and an intense desire to recommend to others. Satisfaction surveys, on the other hand, may be tracking more emotion-laden or sensory service experiences.

The majority of things we buy are acquired with basic needs in mind. If we are evaluating the merits of a new trash compactor, for example, we focus on its reliability, cost, and how effectively it gobbles trash. We don't care if it plays Mozart as trash is crunched or if, out of a sense of loyalty to its owners, it refuses to call the Environmental Protection Agency when inappropriate items are funneled into it. We have little emotional involvement in such purchases.

Think of a service situation when your emotions ran high. Maybe it was your honeymoon, a five-star dining experience, or an attempt to get an organization to correct yet another error on a bill or account statement. Let's assume a market researcher was seeking to gauge your evaluation of one of those experiences. Pulling out his handy-dandy survey, he asks you: "On a scale from 1 to 10, with 1 being 'completely unsatisfied' and 10 being 'completely satisfied,' what would be your overall evaluation of your honeymoon?"

Recalling the full moon on the water, the soft breeze on the balcony, the sweet taste of champagne—or other extracurricular activities—you would likely be struck by how far short "completely satisfied" fell of capturing your true evaluation of that special experience. "Is 'awesome' one of the choices?" you query the interviewer. "No," the surveyor responds. "'Completely satisfied' is our highest rating. We are scientists, not touchy-feely counselors!"

"But you're asking me about an emotional experience," you persist. "Of course we are," pipes the researcher. "We rely on rigorous methods grounded in solid research. And emotional language like 'awesome' clearly has no place in this process. So, just give me a number. Were you satisfied or not?"

On the surface, you might spot an easy route around this grading dilemma. Why not make the top end of the scale "*more than satisfied*?" But the challenge with this path is that "more than" is a different paradigm all together. Satisfaction is about sufficiency, and "more than sufficient" is like saying, "I bought this trash compacter to crunch up my garbage, but if you really want to capture my loyalty as a consumer, make it do something it was not intended to do." Satisfaction is state of completeness—either it is or it is not. If satisfaction were a bucket to be filled, the best you could get would be "completely satisfied"—as in, "to the top."

The rational side of you might be thinking, "But most service experiences are far more ordinary than a honeymoon." Let's examine that belief more closely. The word "service," derived from the Latin *servire*, meaning "to act as a servant," connotes the act of meeting a customer's need or requirement, just as a product does. What is different is that a service experience, in many cases, occurs in a way that involves a more extended human-to-human interaction.

Beyond Survey Questions

When leaders of manufacturing organizations are told that 85 percent of their customers were "completely satisfied" with their trash compactors, it is accurately portrayed as a marketing victory. But if customers give that same "completely satisfied" rating to their last restaurant experience, it would likely signal a grade of "C"—meaning "The restaurant passed; it fulfilled all my 'dining at a restaurant' requirements." But such a grade would by no means cement the customer's loyalty to the restaurant. *This helps to explain why the great majority of customers (some studies show 75 percent) who leave an organization for a competitor, when asked, say they were "satisfied or completely satisfied" with the organization they abandoned.* Satisfaction, it seems, has little correlation to loyalty.

Customers who are merely satisfied remain your customer only as long as everything goes their way. But when something better comes along—other providers temporarily slash prices, or they experience even small service problems—whoosh, off they go to the competition. But loyal customers are a different breed. They don't just come back, they don't simply recommend you, they *insist* that their friends do business with you.

Loyal customers act as a volunteer sales force, championing you to others at home, work, in social circles—and even around the globe via recommendations on blogs, online bulletin boards, and Web sites. And because they feel committed to you and see both emotional and business value in the relationship, they will typically pay more for what they get from you because they are convinced it is worth it.

Because of these higher expectations, they can also be more demanding than the customer who sees himself as simply satisfied. But their enormous impact on the bottom line makes these customers well worth the extra maintenance they may require.

So what do all those "Satisfaction Is Job #1" billboards get you? In the best case, a customer who's willing to give you a try. When that customer walks through your door, the marketing or sales department scores a victory. But the more meaningful measure of success is whether that customer, having taken you for a test drive, comes back for more—and convinces friends, family, business associates, or others to do the same. When you've built that kind of passionate customer base, you've created a marketplace advantage that will be difficult for any competitor to match. Finding that edge is what this book is really all about.

PART ONE

MEET THE LOYALTY CREATORS:
Creators of Remarkable Service

"We're on break!" the warehouse attendant barked in response to the customer's repeated, "Hello! Anybody home?" as he waited for assistance at the service desk. It was the customer's third encounter with apathy that Monday. The first was the coffee shop employee who gave him a curt, "What's good about it?" response to his morning greeting. The next was the gas station owner who offered no verbal response or eye contact as the customer enriched the station's coffers by twenty bucks. And now, "We're on break!"

Apathy comes in many shapes and sizes. It can be complete emotional indifference by the cashier, the sleep-walking actions of a hotel housekeeper, or the wooden sound in the customer service representative's voice. Apathy robs work teams of energy, marriages of romance, and organizations of much-needed service sensitivity. Moreover, it communicates a deadly

1

message of indifference to customers. Continue to spend your money with us or not, says the language of apathy—we're okay either way.

We live in an era of passion larceny. Downsizing has robbed colleagues of colleagues, leaving them hollow. Constant reorganizing has not only reshuffled key alliances, it has stolen valued allegiances. Organizations continue to ratchet up the workloads of already overburdened employees. The heartless hustle for ever-higher profit margins has too often put short-term revenues at center stage and long-term partnerships in the cheap seats. As the soul of the organization is put in a profit-at-all-costs vise, what has been squeezed out is the positive spirit of workers. And it's usually customers who pay the price in the form of robotic, half-hearted, or downright rude service.

An irrational cost-control mentality has replaced a spirit of generosity in today's organizations. "Mean" has taken precedence over "going the extra mile." And taking care of number one has pushed the nobility of serving others to the back of the line. One executive we work with recently observed, "As our country's economy is in an important revival, our workforce is in emotional retraction. We need to renew passion."

So how can leaders turn lethargy into lively? How do you create an organization of passionate, customer-focused professionals whose attitudes and efforts make customers equally zealous about doing business with your company? Read on.

What Is a Loyalty Creator?

Loyalty is a lot like motivation—a spirit housed inside someone. Loyalty can be fostered, created, and nurtured only with the permission of its "owner." It cannot be forced or coerced. Imposed loyalty is manipulation. It leads to compliance that ultimately comes back to bite the imposer while alienating the imposee. Forced loyalty exploits; created loyalty excites. Loyalty Creators are servers that attract loyalty from customers by the way they deliver those experiences that customers value.

Over the next seven chapters you'll be introduced to a number of Loyalty Creators to learn their secrets for creating loyal customers. Each of the seven Loyalty Creators we've chosen to spotlight is someone who "assumes personal responsibility for a great customer experience." While each Loyalty Creator profiled has an area of decided strength, all possess the range of skills to meet a wide variety of customer service challenges. Think of each of the seven as a spirit, style, or manner that can be adopted by any service worker.

Like every person, Loyalty Creators possess diverse traits, but we have chosen to focus on one dominant attribute in each of the seven individuals we feature. The goal shouldn't be to assemble a service team with specialists in each of these seven areas; rather, our purpose is to stress the importance of nurturing each of these skills in every person. It's the combination of these characteristics and attitudes that helps make customers passionately devoted to your organization—and impervious to the siren call of your competitors.

Meet the Loyalty Creators: Creators of Remarkable Service

Loyalty Creators can be as varied as snowflakes, but there is a universal trait that unites them: Each is intensely devoted to providing a positive, beyond-the-ordinary service experience for customers. Some serve in highly visible roles where their efforts and actions directly determine the continued loyalty of customers. Others never touch external customers, yet they significantly impact customers' evaluation of service quality through how they serve their colleagues. Regardless of their role or the type of enterprise they work for, all are in the business of turning customers into evangelists for their organizations.

The Joy Carrier

The Joy Carrier engages customers in a fashion that infects them with pleasure. Egalitarian by nature, he seems to thrive on giving service a personal touch. Customers find him confident, curious, and committed to turning lemons into a lemonade stand!

The Partner

A big fan of group effort, the Partner knows that people care when they share. Her goal in service is to engage the customer in an alliance that yields cooperation and teamwork. She views every service encounter as an opportunity to form a lasting bond and begins all customer service interactions with that end in mind.

The Caretaker

If this Loyalty Creator were an occupation, it would be a superconscientious security guard. Ever-vigilant and armed with a big brother's protective mentality, the Caretaker has an abiding attention to detail and acute loyalty both to the customer and the enterprise. The Caretaker is always on the prowl for a service hiccup in the making.

The Problem Solver

Some might call this Loyalty Creator the serious one! It is not that the Problem Solver is solemn or humorless, it's just that she's got an extra "be responsible" chromosome. Agile and adaptable, the Problem Solver views service not so much as a need to fill as a dilemma to debug. Quick to push the right recovery button when things go wrong, this Loyalty Creator is a service engineer.

The Decorator

Remember the story of the optimistic kid who, dropped in a big pile of horse manure, came up saying, "I know there is a new pony in here somewhere!" That is the essence of the Decorator. This Loyalty Creator values decorating the service experience with magic, mirth, and imagination. More than a "wow" maker, this server is more of a "whoa" maker, often leaving customers with more a sense of awe than of surprise.

The Conscience

Armed with a super-sensitive antenna for any act or attitude that jeopardizes customer trust, the Conscience is a fan of aligned service that yields consistency for the customer. The Conscience is also the fearless devotee of honorable service, the kind that makes customers feel the organization is looking out for their best interests. Always on the hunt for anything that smacks of bureaucracy or hypocrisy, this Loyalty Creator abhors anything that yields an experience customers find unreliable or unethical.

The Giver

The Giver is the Loyalty Creator that serves with the spirit of abundance. This server looks to communicate in a way that leaves customers feeling valued. The Giver is more interested in building long-term relationships than besting customers in one-time interactions. The Giver always seeks win-win agreements with customers.

1
The Joy Carrier

"Enthusiasm is the leaping lightning,
not to be measured by the horse-
power of the understanding."
—RALPH WALDO EMERSON

You can tell you are about to meet a Joy Carrier when a colleague's face lights up just announcing, "Let me get David for you." The coworker's animated look lodges your eager anticipation somewhere between "You are in for a treat" and "You ain't gonna believe this!" Then it happens. You come face-to-face with a person who has fallen hopelessly in love with his role!

We were staying at the Marriott Oak Brook near Chicago, and we had finished a meeting with one client and were en route to a nearby restaurant to meet another client for dinner. While the restaurant was beyond walking distance, it was an insultingly short haul for a taxi driver. But the hotel van was available, and bell stand attendant David Harris was to be our driver.

Now imagine this. You can "feel" David emotionally long before he shakes your hand. His enthusiasm is so apparent that his spirit meets you before he does. The first thing you notice is David's glowing smile—like he unexpectedly encountered two long-lost boyhood friends. The second thing you notice is his gait, a man extremely eager to connect and raring to serve. Finally, you witness how his gusto infects every person within earshot with a robust case of the grins.

"Is it true I get the grand pleasure of being the chauffeur for you gentlemen tonight?" he asked incredulously, like he was still pinching himself after winning a big prize. Depositing us at the restaurant, he gave us each a two-handed shake and his business card. "Would you gentlemen please call me when you finish dinner? I can be here in five minutes! And if you want to bring back a few buddies for a nightcap, we would love to take care of them as well." We literally wanted to rush through dinner just to hurry and get a return visit from the joyful spirit that accompanied David Harris.

The Anatomy of the Joy Carrier

Joy Carriers are easy to spot. Their countenance is brighter than normal; their customer courtship is more confident than usual; and their connection is more captivating than typical. They parade charisma without charging admission. The charm of a Joy Carrier is just there for you to enjoy, with no strings attached.

Joy Carriers are not easily derailed or bothered by people whose experiences have turned them bitter or cynical. Their freedom is not an expression of rebellion or revolt. They show their joyful spirit because that is who they are, not because they have anything to prove.

What is it about this special breed of Loyalty Creator that turns them into Pied Pipers of sorts, making customers want to fall in line behind them in hopes that some of the joyful spirit might rub off? David Harris provides us with the perfect example to explore and understand.

Unconditional Service

The morning after our ride with David, we reflected on the special experience. What had made it so inviting and refreshing? What was it about David that caused us to feel so great about sharing the adventure with him? Was this a serendipitous moment or was this the everyday David? Was this nature, nurture, or the handiwork of some superior manager?

Our first thought was that David was having fun with us, not *for* us or *on behalf of us.* He was not a performer in pursuit of applause or a server eager to win a gratuity. He was just enjoying his role for the pure, simple pleasure it brought to both the served and the server. David obviously enjoyed the effect of his warmth and charisma. Yet it was clear he likely would have had a great time just "playing by himself."

Unbridled Passion

Watching David in action, you get the distinct impression that his mother forgot to tell him to be quiet. He likely was encouraged to laugh as loud and as long as he wanted to, which enabled him to grow up without a built-in governor on his joy level. He no doubt developed a comfort and confidence for expressing joy beyond the boundaries that contain most people. People like David are not generally coached or tutored into being Joy Carriers. They come that way.

This unbridled style has a magnetic power on customers. Being in the presence of David-like employees makes customers feel good about themselves. It's difficult to misbehave or stay cranky in the company of a Joy Carrier.

Rampant Curiosity

Several weeks after our joy ride with David, we encountered him again on a return visit to the hotel. We were waiting for a colleague to join us in the lobby when David walked through the area. His exuberance was just as infectious as we remembered. "You gentlemen going to be here for several days?" he asked, in the same excited manner.

Sensing we had time to kill, David turned up the volume on his curiosity. His questions were constructed more from sincere interest than from subtle intention. He wanted nothing more than to understand us. We found ourselves telling him more than we intended. Joy Carriers are like that. Their complete absence of judgment invites unexplained openness and unexpected candor. Because they come from a place that is unguarded and genuine, they invite the same attitude and response from others.

Benefits and Risks of the Joy Carrier

Joy Carriers remind us of what we all could be absent the reserve and timidity bred into us by socialization, fear of failure, and adulthood. These types of employees generate customer loyalty simply because they are so much fun to be around—a rare commodity amid the grim-faced, bland, or going-through-the-motions customer service employees encountered in so many organizations today. "David sure makes customers smile a lot," one of his colleagues told us.

Joy Carriers also evoke a sense of adventure in customers. As "happiness scouts," they convince us to experiment and entice us to expand our service horizons. Caught up in the fun of the moment, we try that unique entrée we otherwise might have avoided, or we embrace a product color, style, or version we might have formerly thought outside the boundaries of our taste. Persuaded by their confidence and joy in discovering the new, we are jolted out of our routines in ways that renew our spirits and help us see the value of taking calculated risks.

Joy Carriers don't come without a downside. Unchecked, their passion can overstep customers' comfort zones. A sense of freedom can render them fearless when caution is warranted; it happens when they inaccurately assume those around them are caught up in the same exuberance.

Joy Carriers don't always have the self-awareness needed to modify or tone down their styles to match more muted moments or to align with customers' varied service preferences. There are times when clients want or expect order and civility, for example, or when they seek a quiet competence. Joy Carriers may interpret a customer's reserve as their own failure to please through enthusiasm, causing them to ratchet up their jack-in-the-box behavior higher. The result can be viewed as presumptive, even intimidating, when customers expect a more low-key, business-like interaction.

How to Lead a Joy Carrier

Joy Carriers often fare best when partnered with leaders who encourage their exuberant spirit while gently restraining their occasional excesses. Leaders best able to manage a Joy Carrier are those who appreciate their distinctive gifts and understand their atypical manners. Joy Carriers require leaders who nurture their natural gifts as well as alert them to the dangers of turning off customers who prefer their service delivered in hushed tones rather than via jubilant trumpets.

LEADING THE JOY CARRIER

Always be real and authentic.

Tell a Joy Carrier the absolute truth—always.

Make work as fun as possible for the Joy Carrier.

Engage the Joy Carrier with obvious curiosity and keen interest.

Give the Joy Carrier the greatest opportunity possible to be who he is.

Give the Joy Carrier gentle reining-in when he oversteps his bounds.

Yet too much control and conformity will quash what makes them so unique and valuable in creating loyal customers. Ask the Joy Carrier to continually modify or tone down his behavior to match customer preferences, and you risk whittling him down to yet another garden-variety server who does little to excite customer passion. While decorum and by-the-book behavior have their place, odds are you already have plenty of employees who've mastered those rock-like roles.

The challenge for organizations is to keep the special light in Joy Carriers from being turned out. That requires leaders with the courage to both support and shield. As the manager of a Joy Carrier, you must be willing to tolerate the *periodic* excesses of unbridled passion because you understand how vital that attribute is, over the long haul, to enchanting customers and uplifting coworkers.

Joy Carriers' tendency to race too far ahead of prudence means their leaders often need to provide gentle reining-in, like a seasoned jockey might guide a prized racehorse to victory. Jockey Edgar Prado's gentle handling of 2006 Kentucky Derby winner Barbaro had as much to do with humane as it did competitive considerations. When asked why he never used his whip, Prado responded, "If he's running real hard, why should he be punished?" Effective leaders of Joy Carriers harbor the same philosophy.

By the same token, the leader of a Joy Carrier must be generous in his backing to send the message that such infectious employee behavior is encouraged, not frowned upon. Such support signals that Joy Carriers are employees to be emulated, not oddities to be tolerated.

Atmosphere of Authenticity

Joy Carriers thrive in an atmosphere of authenticity. Few cultural characteristics nurture freedom like genuineness. Joy Carriers are free to concentrate all of their energy on the business of delighting customers when they aren't constantly looking over their shoulders. There's no need to spend precious mental or emotional energy trying to figure out spoken innuendo or negotiate political minefields. Such cultures require leaders who don't put up a facade, who readily acknowledge their own weaknesses as well as strengths, and who insist others around them do the same.

Chosen, Not Just Hired

Joy Carriers need to feel valued, not just employed. Their gifts are maximized when given assignments that honor their unique talents, such as cheerleader roles designed to motivate the troops, being asked to host external groups or visiting VIPs, or breaking the ice with employees who are resistant to certain events or tasks.

We were working with the senior leadership team of a client company to help craft a service strategy. Hidden agendas, turf issues, and high-pressured priorities made negotiating the two-day meeting a lot like walking through a minefield. Fortunately, an action team representing a cross-section of company employees had been appointed to assist the executive team with implementation. The team met the day after the executive retreat and demonstrated the open, passionate spirit the execs had lacked—the team was populated with Joy Carriers. When the team joined the executive group at its next off-site meeting, the energy was dramatically different and the results of the combined teams nothing short of spectacular. More proof that the spirit of Joy Carriers is highly contagious!

Celebrate Eccentricity

Joy Carriers are usually characters, and David is no exception. Character translates to unusual or eccentric, and in the traditional view of order-laden organizational life that often means an entity to be shunned. But the truth is that many great organizations have been created by eccentric individuals whose personalities fell outside the mainstream.

Look at the founders of Turner Broadcasting, Apple Computer, Virgin Airlines, Netflix, Southwest Airlines, and others and you'll find people who were labeled "crazy" or even "insane" by pundits, analysts, academics, and competitors. Talk to anyone who's done something provocative within an organization—who has upset the apple cart by creating new ways of doing business or who has bent a rule in the name of pleasing customers—and you'll often find that someone labeled as "weird" or "loony." They are characters in the purest sense of the word: individuals often focused on bringing new heart and soul to enthusiasm-averse coworkers operating on autopilot around them.

We believe it's important that borderline eccentricity be celebrated, not just for the affirmation of passion but for how casting such a spotlight communicates "We value this!" Oak Brook Marriott Hotel manager Ted Selogie puts it this way: "I would never say, 'Go be David.' I would instead suggest, 'Let your spirit come out like David is able to do.'"

Like a team mascot working the hometown crowd into a frenzy, Ted is inviting spirit more than affirming David. In so doing, he is creating the conditions for the kind of happy eccentricity that customers often find so magnetic—and that makes them look forward to returning again and again to bask in the glow of the Joy Carrier.

The Partner

It's hard to describe how an ordinary customer service experience morphs into a *partner* experience. It might start with a polite, respectful, and obviously deferential interaction. While such treatment might not evoke a "customer as king" feeling, you clearly know you are being served by someone noticeably sensitive to your evaluation. The shift to a partner experience might be triggered by a joke, a special request, or perhaps a candid answer to a targeted question. You went from being served to being invited to co-create an experience—and it's yours!

Customers know what to expect in dialogues filled with "May I take your order?" or "Smoking or nonsmoking?" or "Take a seat and we'll call you." But a good partnering experience feels foreign, yet in a wholly welcome and positive way.

What does the Loyalty Creator we call the Partner look like up close and personal?

We were working with a client in Puerto Rico. Arriving at the Ritz-Carlton San Juan midday, we checked in and made our way to one of the hotel's restaurants. Jennifer Lacomba had a menu in our hands before our bottoms touched our seats. Her sprawling warmth enveloped us like sunrise on a spring morning. "I am so glad you are dining with me," she said. Her manner was a perfect blend of the attentiveness of a grand host and the confidence of someone with complete dominion over her service environment.

"Where are you boys from?" she asked, smartly adjusting her style to be in sync with our way-too-obvious Southern accents. When our answers conveyed a willingness to be playful, she followed our lead.

She was an authority on the menu, frank and forthcoming on what items she liked and those she wasn't so fond of. Her authenticity elicited our unreserved trust in her menu recommendations. Finding that we were interested in cuisine slightly off the beaten path, she took the clue and ran.

"You want to try my special sauce with those French fries? It gets rave reviews from the brave souls willing to give it a try." Her expression was both impish and certain—this was clearly her playground and she had all the toys! We enthusiastically took the bait.

We watched her do what distinguishes all great Partners—use inclusion as a platform for delivering exemplary service. She refilled our iced tea without request and asked us to give her assistance moving a heavy table nearby. She brought more dinner rolls and briefly sat down with us at our table to solicit feedback when she brought our check.

But her partnering efforts didn't end with the check. When we gathered our stuff to leave, instead of inviting us back, she kept the partnership going. "Can we do this again tomorrow?" she asked, like she'd had as much fun as we had. Jennifer was not our waitress—she was our partner in creating an extraordinary service experience.

Inside the Mind of the Partner

Service delivered by the Partner is scriptless service squared. If we disassembled the "Jennifer" brand to examine its parts, we would find a collection of highly adaptable service skills; she obviously had more interpersonal tools in her arsenal than partnering acumen. Had we been a more somber pair of guests searching for a quiet place that required a low-energy investment in the functional act of eating, we undoubtedly would have gotten a different Jennifer.

Jennifer, as a server first and delighter second, took her cues from us. She never reached beyond our banter, and she used pitch-perfect queries to gauge our receptiveness to play partner. She never abandoned her core service duties to simply chit chat.

Think of a partnership spirit as an overlay on the basic requirements for good service, a value-add that lifts the average service encounter to new heights. We *expected* hot rolls— but we were *enchanted* by Jennifer's playful, inclusive attitude.

Jennifer's confidence emanated from a space of self-esteem, not from the repertoire of a trained actress. It's difficult to teach scriptless service through training drills or memorization exercises; much of it is extemporaneous service straight from the heart. Jennifer-like self-assurance requires an adventurous spirit, a supportive environment, and relatively hands-off supervision. While the very essence of service is "to give," the Partner does more *gifting* than giving. Giving implies a tit-for-tat component: I gave you something of value, now you have an opportunity to return the favor. Gifting, on the other hand, suggests doing something for the sheer joy of giving and the pleasure of watching the response. With gifting, reciprocity is solely in the reaction of the receiver—there is no expectation of future payback.

Jennifer was not motivated purely by the potential of a large tip. While the extra money is always nice, what really drives and sustains her—why she comes to work each day—is the feeling she receives when customers react positively to the warmth and partnering spirit she emanates.

Invitation to Participate

The core of partnership is inclusion. The Partner knows how and when to invite customers to co-create the experience. Look again at Jennifer's mischievous invitation: "You want to try my special sauce with those French fries? It gets rave reviews from the brave souls willing to give it a try." She offered something unique—and she offered it with pride. Most of us are suckers for a special offering, especially when it feels custom-made and is seasoned with a big helping of confidence and pride. And who could resist accepting her challenge to become a member of the "brave souls" club?

Partnering requires strong self-esteem. Insecure servers will be derailed by any rejection of an invitation to partner, becoming hesitant to make such efforts again. Partners take great pride in both their role and their charge. They exude knowingness in the fact that they are good at what they do and they don't need a customer to confirm their competence. Insecure servers search for signals that they are good enough, keeping them in a subservient position rather than the "we're-all-equals-here" stance essential to effective partnering.

Some partnering invitations are more risky than others, of course. Requests that smack of controlling behavior usually do more to repel than to recruit. Had Jennifer simply brought us a dish of her special sauce and insisted we try it, we might have politely declined. Guilt-laced invites have a similar track record. "It really would be good for you to try my . . ." would have evoked memories of Mom pushing us to "eat our vegetables" while we eyed a pie baking in the oven. Good partnering requires a mellow draw—not a muscled demand.

Comfort with Give and Take

The Partner is a highly elastic and adaptable creature. We know that if our spirited exchange with Jennifer had suddenly turned more serious or business-like, she would have adjusted without uncertainty or unease. A partnering spirit is about affirming relationships more through ebb and flow than give and take. Instead of nitpicking details, the Partner works to roll with anticipated imperfections—or unexpected waves of discontent.

Generosity-Driven

It's rare to find a good Partner who keeps score. The noncompetitive nature of effective partnering means that each partner approaches the customer relationship believing not that there is a finite quantity of benefit to be derived, but that giving ever more to the relationship causes it to grow and prosper.

The Partner gives without conditions. It is service emanating from the inner joy of serving, not a calculated decision. It requires a focus not on short-term financial benefit, but on long-term relationship value. While transaction costs are not irrelevant, they can become destructively dominant. Partners understand that by seeking win-win solutions and avoiding nickel-and-diming customers to death, their organization will be rewarded with grateful and devoted customers who return again and again, often with friends or family in tow.

Benefits and Drawbacks of the Partner

Partnering with customers can be a mixed blessing. The good news is that when done well, it engenders intimacy and stimulates loyalty. Customers made to feel like lifetime partners are more committed to the organization and are often more forgiving of mistakes; the nature of the relationship creates a less hypercritical appraisal of service. Partner-like customers—those who feel that an organization has their best interests at heart—buy more, buy more frequently, advocate more, forgive more, and trust more than transactional customers.

Like the Joy Carrier, the Partner is not without disadvantages. Partnering behavior raises the expectations of customers and demands a greater investment of emotional energy than more run-of-the-mill service interactions. Consider the relationships you have with a significant other or best friend. Investing so much in their well-being—listening, advising, and always being there in times of need—can eventually lead to burnout. Much like personal relationships, even the best customer partnerships experience their share of strains and challenges.

Service leaders must stay vigilant for signs of server wear. Symptoms of burnout can include a flat edge to communications, reactions that indicate dullness or slowness when the opposite is the norm, a short fuse with customers, or a martyr-like attitude expressed as the refusal of help or support from teammates.

How to Foster "Partnering" Performance

What can organizations and leaders do to help facilitate and encourage the extraordinary partnering spirit demonstrated by the Jennifers of the world? What are the props or supporting elements that help ensure award-winning partnering performance?

Exemplary partnering starts with a clear service vision. A vision is the guiding beacon that employees follow to ensure they're delivering the kind of service that sets them apart from the competition; it's the service policies, processes, and protocols unique to an organization.

Good partners also need broad guidelines that give them "solution spaces" in which to operate—a form of decision tree to help make appropriate (and customer friendly) decisions in a variety of service situations. High-level partnering also requires the knowledge that mistakes won't be fatal; that missteps in the pursuit of delighting customers will be viewed as learning experiences, not handled with punitive measures. Finally, front-line workers need the appropriate coaching and feedback to fine-tune their partnering skills. Let's look at each of these elements in more detail.

Provide Vision and Purpose

Ritz-Carlton San Juan Hotel put Jennifer through an orientation program that communicated to her the hotel's vision of "ladies and gentlemen serving ladies and gentlemen." The Ritz-Carlton Hotel Company has long understood that employees can't be expected to deliver first-rate customer service if leadership can't first define it. As retired Ritz-Carlton Hotel Company president Horst Schulze was fond of telling associates, "Elegance without warmth is arrogance." But Jennifer's on-boarding featured much more than learning catchy slogans. She was taught the hotel's particular version of service excellence: creating a warm, relaxed yet refined ambiance for guests.

Latitude for Interpersonal Experimentation

The Partner is at her best operating under flexible guidelines, not lock-step marching orders. The formula for good partnering is the absence of formula. Partnering is an attitude that emanates from the heart. It is sculpted by a set of values and propelled by a love of serving. The Partner requires freedom to shape customer relationships in ways she deems appropriate for the situation. Jennifer was inventive because she couldn't help it—and because someone gave her the latitude to express that natural gift.

LEADING THE PARTNER

Remind the Partner of your organization's vision for service.

Anchor directions to company purpose and mission.

Provide broad guidelines, not restrictive procedures.

Support and correct the Partner when her risk-taking backfires.

Teach her through anecdotes and examples.

Be the partner to her that you want her to be to customers.

Praise the Partner's initiative and excellence, not just her results.

Protocols: Coupling Responsibility with Freedom

Protocols are the service norms and practices unique to given organizations. Interpersonal exchange protocols, for example, offer guidelines for communication practices with customers. Jennifer knew that the distinctive Ritz-Carlton service experience required use of refined language with guests ("my pleasure") rather than colloquialisms ("no problem"). She also knew that she was expected to honor a set of standards ("Any employee who receives a guest complaint 'owns' the complaint until it is resolved") integral to the Ritz-Carlton Hotel Company service vision. A Partner operates with a free form, not a wild form.

Protection: Support for "Failing on Purpose"

Script-less service can be a high-risk venture. There is a risk the customer will misread a friendly style. There is also a chance the server will become too familiar or friendly with guests, overstepping what customers see as proper or professional behavior. A vital prop for the Partner is support and encouragement from managers should an experiment in partnering fail to work. Coaching should focus on helping servers make good decisions on when to push forward and when to pull back based on customer cues. Leaders should also stress that partnering skills are rarely mastered on the first few attempts to use them.

The Partner represents an attitude and an orientation that starts with a deep respect for the customer and a spirit of collaboration; the Partner doesn't rest until every effort has been made to exceed expectations. It comes from recognition that great service is more often than not a co-creation—by the server in concert with the served.

3 The Caretaker

"Give all thou canst; high heaven
rejects the lore of nicely-calculated
less or more."

—WILLIAM WORDSWORTH

Host. The word carries a variety of meanings, each painted in the color "help." It conjures a maitre d' escorting a guest to the best table, a hotel concierge taking the stress out of a tourist's holiday, or an exposition hall manager ensuring no detail is overlooked in preparing for an upcoming conference.

Steve Win doesn't work at a restaurant, hotel, or convention hall, but he is the consummate host. Steve is a chauffeur in Chicago. Although "chauffeur" is the occupation listed on his tax return, "caretaker" is the preoccupation displayed in his job. He operates his business under the banner of "Win Signature Service." These three words—win-signature-service—speak volumes about Steve.

John landed at Chicago O'Hare Airport earlier than expected and called Steve cell-to-cell; Steve just happened to be in the parking garage at O'Hare. He suggested John walk to baggage claim because Steve could meet him there a lot faster than by driving out of the garage and getting snarled in incoming airport traffic. He called John a few minutes later to make sure he was departing at the United Airlines' baggage claim door; a second, out-of-breath call followed on its heels (Steve had sprinted from the parking garage to the United baggage claim area) to make sure he had not missed John. As John exited the terminal at the prescribed spot, there was a smiling Steve Win eager to shake hands.

Steve is always early for appointments. His car is immaculate. He handles his passengers' luggage as if he were handling a crate of eggs. He always greets customers with a large smile, a handshake, and a very warm greeting. We never have to ask him to adjust the heat or air conditioning; he just seems to know the correct temperature for us. If we call him from one of our cell phones, he sees the number and answers, "Hello, Dr. Bell, how are you, sir?" If he is unavailable to pick up one or both of us, he makes arrangements with a fellow driver to fill in—and each, without fail, has the same friendly manner and fastidious attention to detail.

The Caretaker is intensely loyal to a customer. Read that line again and pay attention to the singular predicate. Caretakers do not think of the target of their service efforts in plural . . . they only think in singular. When you are around Steve Win, he seems completely absorbed in you and you alone. The truth is that he is processing a million details as he works to ensure that clients get from here to there on time. But all of that is kept behind the scenes. All customers see and feel is a laser-like, in-the-moment focus on their unique needs and concerns.

The Caretaker Profile

Caretakers are service choreographers—not unlike a host, they know a great customer experience requires managing an amalgamation of diverse elements. Fail on even one performance dimension, and it can color the whole experience negatively for customers. A waitress might be warm and friendly, but if she can't get orders right or remember the daily specials, her weaknesses will overshadow her strengths. The call-center phone representative might be knowledgeable and efficient, but if he has little patience for customer problems or is short with coworkers, his product knowledge is lost amid the interpersonal flaws.

Effective service choreography requires integration, organization, and alignment; it means mastering the little things and managing the customer's experience from end to end. Like seasoned event planners, they manage the flow and pace of the experience—the ease, agility, and effectiveness of service.

Caretakers also "backward serve." They have a clear picture of what the outcome should be, then work backward from that goal to ensure the reality matches the vision. They also have a sixth sense for anticipating what can go wrong in service encounters. They set out to ensure the experience *product* matches the experience *plan*. The Caretaker knows that it's not the lions and tigers that usually doom service quality, it is the gnats and mosquitoes—those tiny irritants that are easy to overlook but often deliver pain or aggravation out of proportion to their size.

Five Paths to Drag-Free Service

In studying Steve Win-like servers, we have found five recurring traits that distinguish the Caretaker style and help to create devoted customers. Caretakers we've encountered regularly share the following characteristics:

#1: They create made-to-order service experiences

"Let me show you a shortcut" or "You might want to do it like this" or "If you call right after lunch, you will have a much better chance . . ." are comments that customers are likely to hear from the Caretaker. Caretakers believe every customer should be treated like the *only* customer. They are forever on the hunt for ways to make the customer's experience go smoothly, without encumbrance or drag.

#2: They plan well and show resourcefulness

Steve Win plots our driving route with the kind of preparation that would impress a military intelligence unit. Armed with the latest information on weather, traffic flow, time of day, and alternate routes—knowledge updated by his "scouts" along the way—he ensures our experience is hassle-free. His prior planning enables him to ensure we experience minimal drag in each and every service experience.

#3: They are masters of detail

Caretakers remember the little things about customers. They make mental notes of preferences so they can improve service on the next encounter. They are always on the prowl for ideas or small tokens of appreciation they can give to customers to make them feel special. They know that sense of caring and special attention builds a bond that becomes difficult to break.

#4: They view policies and processes through the eyes of customers

Caretakers are often the first to object when an organization introduces a new policy or procedure that may make life more difficult for customers. They don't see the customer through the lens of the organization; they see the organization through the lens of the customer. They abhor concepts like "acceptable error rate," "adequate," or "satisfactory," preferring "precision," "error-free," and "excellence" instead. They can quickly size up a prospective service interaction, spot the weak links or breakdowns waiting to happen, and adjust accordingly. Hand a Caretaker a broken or flawed service process, and he can usually offer practical ways to repair it or make it more user-friendly—a skill that makes him a valuable addition to any service-improvement task force.

#5: They are voracious learners and effective teachers

Caretakers are eager learners who are always looking for ways to make things work better. They are usually the first to know what competitors are up to, and they often have their own special methods for delivering good service.

Caretakers also can be gifted instructors. They turn many customer relationships into opportunities to teach—not so they can show off their expertise, but because they genuinely want to offer help, be it by offering a time or money-saving tip or another piece of advice. They know that if they instruct customers, they will be instructed *by* their customers in how to provide the most effective service.

Pros and Cons of the Caretaker

As the self-proclaimed "voice of the customer," the Caretaker can offer valuable perspectives and insights that help organizations better understand customer needs and preferences. They are often a valuable source for ideas on eliminating process factors that cause customers to view companies as difficult to do business with. Caretakers that we've studied also are important bellwethers that can alert units or organizations to weak spots in service delivery systems—and help head off customer defections.

However, Caretakers are often perfectionists. Their perpetual search for better ways to do business can grate on colleagues who just want to get the job done.

Managing the Caretaker

Caretakers do not need a lot of tender loving care or hands-on managing. They find solace in their work and reward in their achievement. They would rather figure things out for themselves than be told how something is done. Caretakers are more "arrangers and providers" than "entertainers and performers," and the way they are managed and coached should reflect that difference.

LEADING THE CARETAKER

Listen to the Caretaker.

Be generous with your time; be gentle with your advice.

Caretakers love feedback but loathe evaluation. Focus on the future.

Show emotion with the Caretaker.

Build trust with the Caretaker.

Mentoring is an effective way to support the Caretaker. But since Caretakers love to teach as much as to learn, mentoring can't only be a one-way, master-to-novice transaction. To be effective, the mentoring process must be designed and managed as a two-way partnership, the synchronized efforts of two people seeking to learn from another. A mentoring partnership is about teaching through consultation rather than through constriction, awareness rather than assessment.

Leaders who mentor effectively value humility over arrogance, collaboration over control. They zero in on future promise rather than dwelling on past mistakes or actions. They listen to learn, not to look for opportunities to lecture or show off their knowledge. They provide support for the Caretaker by building learning opportunities into the position and the work environment. And they are always on the hunt for resources that can expand the competence, confidence, and capacity of the Caretaker.

The Caretaker's "Value Add"

The most productive way to take care of the Caretaker is by providing the tools (or access to the tools) needed for effective performance. Caretakers are service tinkerers. And to tinker, one needs tinker toys. Steve Win not only has the usual chauffeur gear—umbrella, GPS, PDA, cell phone, maps, flashlight, first aid kit—he sports an additional toolkit that helps him take his service to another level and keep customers coming back for more. He has refreshments, newspapers, and magazines for passengers. Ask about a play, movie, or sports event in town, and just like a hotel concierge he has the latest directory at his fingertips. Inquire about a type of restaurant, and he can recommend several at any price range that you request. Steve also has an array of local experts—friends, business associates, and other regular customers—ready to assist at his beck and call.

The Value of Patient Leadership

Patience and flexibility are vital traits when it comes to effectively leading Steve-like servers. The Caretaker's focus on details and minutiae can sometimes test leaders more comfortable with broad-brush strategic thinking. But Caretakers thrive under elastic leadership styles, not tolerant ones. Elasticity suggests a relationship with give and flex, one that expands to accommodate. Tolerance-based relationships are usually exercises in sufferance. Tolerant leaders are perpetually pained by the imperfections they see, but they usually suffer silently without comment. There is a resignation, as in, "This unfortunate disruption or personality quirk just comes with the territory." Leaders who manage Caretakers well don't recoil at small glitches; they roll with unexpected jabs and demonstrate expansive, don't-sweat-the-small-stuff attitudes.

Steve Win, for example, is a perfectionist, not perfect. Yet even during an incident of imperfection, his devotion to the customer enabled him to turn a moment of disdain into a memory of delight. John was en route to the Hyatt Hotel in Rosemont, Illinois, a short distance from the Chicago O'Hare airport. He was unaware, however, that there were two Hyatts in the O'Hare area. Steve delivered him to the wrong one. By the time John made the discovery, Steve had disappeared into the night. Realizing the right hotel was only blocks away, John had a taxi drive him the short distance.

A few hours later, Chip landed en route to the same Hyatt Hotel as John. Since John had e-mailed Chip a note on his Blackberry about the hotel mix-up, Steve learned of his error when Chip gave him the address of a different Hyatt. Steve instantly called John on his cell phone to provide a sincere apology. He offered to reimburse John for his taxi fare and suggested that his next trip be "on the house."

It was obvious that Steve was more pained than John was inconvenienced. Caretakers are like that. Above all else, they care! It's a magic formula that turns customer apathy into customer devotion.

The Problem Solver

Freeman®, a company headquartered in Dallas, Texas, provides services for exhibitions, conventions, and corporate events. Attend any large trade show around the country, and odds are Freeman has supplied much of the furnishings and merchandise you see around you.

Exhibitors at trade shows evaluate Freeman on whether they receive what they ordered and whether the display merchandise arrives at their exhibit booths on time and without damage. With hundreds of moving parts involved, managing an exposition hall requires the precision of a Swiss watch and the timing of a crackerjack pit crew.

Despite its best efforts, Freeman wasn't satisfied with the service quality it provided customers; in particular, management wanted to improve how the company resolved customer problems. Integral to the effort was the creation of a special-forces team trained to solve the problems and restore the confidence of disappointed or angry exhibitors. The brainchild behind the concept was Keith Kennedy, Problem Solver extraordinaire.

Keith Kennedy recently retired from Freeman after more than forty years in operations. However, he is still renowned throughout the trade-show industry for his ability to quickly diagnose and solve complex service problems and soothe anxieties in ways that restore customer trust and generate repeat business.

Consider an example of Keith's troubleshooting handiwork. At the close of each trade show, every exhibitor was asked to handwrite bills of lading for each shipment leaving the convention facility; it required writing out labels for every crate, carton, or case that was to be shipped. Many exhibitors spent hours filling out documents and labels. Acutely aware of the grief this was causing customers, Keith developed a program that would print the documents for every customer and deliver them to each booth. Customers were ecstatic. But the best was yet to come. When customers inquired about the charge for the new service, they were told it was free! The gratis component was Keith's idea as well. Freeman thus became the first contractor in the industry to offer a document preparation service.

The Problem Solver Profile
The Loyalty Creator we call the Problem Solver is a world-class "unraveler." His mission is to remove any pain or hassle

from the customer's experience. Like a character in the *Mission Impossible* movies, the Problem Solver views his work world as a series of puzzles. Where others throw up their hands, the Problem Solver quickly dives in and seeks solutions. This variety of Loyalty Creator exhibits a single-minded focus on solving the problem, often wasting little time reading owner's manuals or instructions. Problem Solvers often have an eager impatience about their nature. Yet that restlessness doesn't translate to being trigger-happy or impulsive. On the contrary, the decisions and actions of Problems Solvers like Keith are usually grounded in substance and driven by solid information and life experience. Their edginess simply reflects an action orientation. Thinking of ways to improve the customer's experience keeps them up at night; anticipating or correcting service hiccups is their lifeblood.

Unlike the Joy Carrier, Partner, and Caretaker, who tend to wear their emotions on their sleeves, the Problem Solver is more understated. Part engineer and part inventor, these employees possess a more subtle nature that can conceal their intentions and mask their manners. What is unmistakable, however, is their obsession with delivering exemplary customer service—particularly when it comes to heading off or fixing service breakdowns. Three behavioral characteristics mark the Problem Solver and contribute to his uncanny ability to stimulate customer loyalty.

#1: They put out fires

The Problem Solver exhibits ingenuity and decisive action in repairing customer service experiences gone wrong. This

Loyalty Creator knows it's not enough to fix the problem. He also has to fix the customer, who is often in a state of high anxiety—or white-hot anger—following service mishaps.

The Problem Solver knows that a service fire is not extinguished until the customer's emotional state is returned to neutral, at a minimum. This usually requires letting the customer tell his side of the story—and vent if needed—without making excuses, interrupting with corrections, or pointing fingers. Emotional repair also demands a heartfelt apology (regardless of who's to blame for the problem) and a show of empathy. As an executive for a prominent technology company once told us, "The upset customer doesn't care how much you know until he knows how much you care."

Problem Solvers also know that it's important to follow up on actions taken in the heat of the battle. They circle back to inspect the customer's temperament after the embers of the fire have dissipated; they know that follow-up is the customer's most believable proof of concern.

"Keith Kennedy has the tenacity and determination to get the job done no matter what it takes," says Don Freeman, CEO of Freeman. "When it's late at night and others want to stop and come back in the morning, Keith is the one who says 'There will be new fires in the morning; let's put this one out tonight.'"

#2: They nudge (or push) things in the right direction
An electric cattle prod helps a cowboy create a smooth, uninterrupted movement of a herd of cows into a stall or onto a truck. Without the low-voltage shock, a bashful cow

can suddenly turn or do an about-face in the cattle chute, creating a bottleneck or inciting mayhem among the rest of the herd.

Problem Solvers are human cattle prods, ensuring service happens without disturbance or interruption. Like a cowboy sensing the indecision of a steer, they can spot and contain a crisis-in-the-making without customers ever realizing how close they came to disaster. Problem Solvers are usually three moves ahead of the pack.

Creating shipping arrangements with transportation carriers at show sites often created major bottlenecks for exhibitors. Like trying to drive out of a packed parking lot after a ball game, it was a logistical nightmare that often left exhibitors frustrated at the end of a successful show. Keith Kennedy devised a way to break the logjam. Exhibitors could simply call or fax the Freeman call center, or any Freeman branch office, in advance of a show (or the service desk at show site) and arrange for Freeman to handle all of their transportation needs. Working with Freeman branches and partnering with over-the-road and airfreight carriers, Keith created a new service called Exhibit Transportation. Despite the claims of naysayers who doubted it would work, the service has not only become a customer favorite, it makes Freeman a tidy profit.

#3: They repel problems

Problem Solvers are skilled at doing preventive maintenance on the machinery of the customer's service experience. They are campaigners for the preservation and upkeep of the service processes that are required for effective service delivery. Not ones to skim the surface, they rely on analysis to get to the root cause of problems. Suggest a Band-Aid to "just get by," and the Problem Solver will take issue. He is an advocate for enduring solutions and post-mortem evaluations that help stamp out recurring service problems.

The Problem Solver Balance Sheet

What is a Problem Solver's biggest contribution to an organization? We believe it's the way these Loyalty Creators help others understand and embrace the power of creative problem-solving. When people at Freeman say, "How would Keith handle this?" it is less about the man and more about a mindset. It is an attention-to-details perspective that helps colleagues to be more proactive and customer-centric in their execution—and to understand the value of owning customer problems until they are solved. It's about being more attentive to process maintenance and more perceptive in envisioning things that could potentially go wrong in service encounters.

Problem Solvers do have a few foibles. Like bulldozers without braking mechanisms, they can make colleagues crazy with their relentless obsession to preserve, protect, and defend customers from flawed service processes. With their laser-like, in-the-moment focus, they can sometimes miss the forest for the trees. Ignoring an organization's political realities, they can misjudge how their colleagues perceive their intentions.

During a discussion among Freeman's senior leaders about service effectiveness, Keith emphatically stated, "We

should just do away with the customer service desk altogether." His assertion disclosed a deep belief that customer
service should be the responsibility of each and every Freeman representative on the exhibit floor, not just employees
working the convention center service desk. Keith's bold
statement illustrates the mindset of many Problem Solvers. If they believe something can be done to improve the
customer experience, they usually won't hesitate to say it—
regardless of whose feathers are ruffled.

Solving the Problem Solver

The word "guidon" comes from the French meaning "to
guide." It is an expression familiar to anyone with ties to the
military. It refers to the individual who carries the battle flag
into combat, typically at the front of the flank. Battle flags
also evoke commitment to a mission as well as allegiance to
the unit. Problem Solvers need leaders who carry the flag,
helping the Problem Solver to view his narrower problem
through the lens of a broader purpose—particularly company objectives.

The Problem Solver's need to repair what is broken is
a vital part of who he is—almost compulsively so at times.
The Problem Solver needs a leader who can help him focus
his efforts as he can quickly become myopic in his quest to
unsnarl details. Good leaders prompt the Problem Solver
to keep his eye on the long view and not be seduced by a
quick fix.

"Some of our best people used to complain we had too
many goals and initiatives," says Banco Popular North

America President Roberto R. Herencia. "We helped reduce that concern by sharpening and clarifying our focus. We now have one mission and one service vision, supported by four strategic directions (we call them pillars—People, Performance, Customers, and Community), each with a handful of key goals we call shared agreements. By continually anchoring every objective and task back to the mission-vision-pillars-agreements, we not only get alignment, we help keep people from getting distracted fighting alligators and forgetting they were there to drain the swamp."

LEADING THE PROBLEM SOLVER

Keep the organizational vision front and center, not just on the break-area wall.

Let the Problem Solver see the vision through your priorities and practices.

Remind the Problem Solver of the main concerns when he gets side-tracked by the squeaky wheel.

Advocate for the Problem Solver's philosophy even if you cannot back his tactics.

Problem Solvers need tools. Be generous in providing the very best.

The job of leaders is to communicate a clear vision and provide the passion, tools, and support to help others make it happen—then step out of their way. Leaders must have a crystal clear sense of destination, a vivid picture in their head of the end game, then being unwavering in its pursuit.

"Keith believed that great customer service was hand-made at the front line," says Freeman's Katy Wild. "He reminded customer contact employees that they were the most important people in the company. One year he loaded every customer service person in the company on a bus and transported them to his East Texas ranch for a barbecue. It was just one of his many efforts to live his vision of taking care of the customer by taking care of the front line."

Leader As Aligner

Problem Solvers can get easily distracted; they often engage in tactical service battles without regard for the broader strategic war. They need service leaders who can gently nudge them back on course by reminding them of higher-priority goals.

Steve Kabel, Southern California Regional President for John Laing Homes, holds up a copy of *The Little Laing Book* at his quarterly all-hands meeting. The book is given to every employee at orientation and contains the company's credo, mission, principles, and so on. "Never forget we are here to deliver the best new home experience to our customers—one that sets the standard for our industry. When you are tempted to cut corners, miss on a promise, or fail to call the customer back, it may seem to you like an unimportant blemish, but it jeopardizes our mission and tarnishes our reputation."

Leaders need to be masters at front-end alignment. Max DePree, retired CEO of Herman Miller, a leading office furniture manufacturer, wrote in his best-selling book *Leadership Is an Art*, "The first job of the leader is to create reality and the last job is to say 'thank you.'" Leaders as aligners advocate addressing customers' quiet-but-crucial "Priority A's" before getting sidetracked by the noisy-but-trivial "C's."

Leader As Translator

Problem Solvers speak the language of resolution. Some people live in the future; some live in the present. These characters keep a foot firmly in both worlds. Their orientation is not "is" or "will be" but rather "in process." They probably use more gerunds (words ending in "ing") than most people. That mindset requires leaders who understand and appreciate the Problem Solver's special manner of communicating. Freeman CEO Don Freeman would regularly voice affirmation of Keith Kennedy with phrases like, "I completely agree with what Keith is trying to say" or "The philosophy behind what Keith is talking about is important to our success." His role as translator encouraged others to give a fair hearing to Keith's underlying concepts, but stopped short of rubber-stamping all of his specific ideas.

Translator means more than simply interpreting vocabulary. It means fostering understanding in the broadest sense. Leaders as translators encourage Problem Solvers to involve others when they might see going it alone as more efficient or hassle-free. As catalysts of collaboration, they prompt the Problem Solver's colleagues to "go talk with Keith about that situation and get his ideas." They also ensure the Problem Solver's unique solutions get wide circulation as a means of validating the character and affirming the contributions. Leaders as translators know that the more people who get up close and personal with a Problem Solver, the more proficient a unit or organization will become at predicting and troubleshooting service breakdowns.

Leader As Umpire

There is an old baseball story about a batter who, after hearing the pitched ball hit the catcher's mitt, turned to the umpire and asked: "Is it a ball or is it a strike?" The umpire responded without emotion, "It ain't nothing till I call it!" The story is sometimes used to illustrate the sanctity of the umpire. But it really is an example of the necessity of rule enforcers in situations where verdicts concerning justice are not always cut and dried.

Problem Solvers are big fans of improvisation and inventiveness. When seeking solutions to a customer problem, they can sometimes travel outside the boundaries of accepted practices and regulations. If you add necessity to expeditious, you have the mother *and* father of invention. For a Problem Solver, being effective trumps being proper; getting it done outweighs following procedure. In most cases, they see the ends as justifying the means. When Keith made the bold statement about "eliminating the customer service desk altogether" in the middle of a senior leadership discussion about service effectiveness on the exhibit hall floor, he was focused on how best to serve the customer rather than on what might be the most politically correct statement in light of who was in attendance at the meeting. His tendency was to move boldly and quickly in the name of the customer. Keith understood the need to "pilot" such a revolutionary change, but he would need guidance as to how best to implement an effective solution consistently across a nation-wide operation.

This isn't to suggest that leaders need to police the actions of Problem Solvers with the vigilance of private detectives. Most Problem Solvers are neither devious nor unethical in their practices. They simply benefit from leaders who, like great umpires, have the courage to draw the line when they see actions that are imprudent, improper, or that flaunt the rules. With proper guidance, Problem Solvers can become some of the most valuable Loyalty Creators on your team.

5

The Decorator

"The creative act, the defeat of habit
by originality, overcomes everything."

—GEORGE LOIS

Legend has it that in the mid-1600s, when Dom Perignon invented what we know today as champagne, he called to his friends and exclaimed, "Come quickly, I am tasting the stars!" Catalyst Ranch is a place where people go to "taste the stars."

Catalyst Ranch is a meeting and event space in Chicago. But unlike most meeting facilities, Catalyst Ranch was constructed and choreographed for the express purpose of cultivating creativity and birthing breakthrough ideas. Companies like Kraft and Pfizer use the facility to brainstorm about new products; consulting firms like Accenture and McKinsey use it for strategic planning; and retail giants like Whirlpool and DaimlerChrysler favor it as a site for marketing innovation. Room sizes range from 700 to more than 3,000 square feet and can be configured any way the customer desires. Groups of up to 125 people can be accom-modated, and restrooms are a mere eleven steps from any meeting room.

Every room is adorned in outlandish colors and stocked with furniture that might have fallen off the back of a gypsy caravan. You expect magicians, mystics, and juggling clowns to come out of the woodwork. Refreshments and meals range from the unique to the bizarre. The whole ensemble is designed to lift customers out of the pothole of routine and elevate them into a playpen of creative idea generation. Catalyst Ranch operates under the belief that one of the best ways to open the mind is to disorient it—and disoriented you are when you walk into the facility and see all the elements that would never appear in a traditional meeting setting. Log on to *www.catalystranch.com* for a taste of this fantasyland.

The founder of this unique think-tank-for-hire is a shin-ing example of the Loyalty Creator we call the Decorator. Her Web site photo shows her donning a funky, fuzzy bright red hat. Her Web site self-description reads as follows:

Name	Eva Niewiadomski
Title	Ranch Czarina
Favorite vacation site	Thailand
Favorite color	Chartreuse or tangerine
Favorite mode of transportation	Unicycle
Favorite dessert	Mom's rhubarb punch
Favorite recreation	Dancing the salsa
Favorite quote	"If you think you are too small to have an impact, try to go to bed with a mosquito." —Anita Roderick

Eva Niewiadomski is not the eccentric leader you'd expect to find in such a nontraditional setting. Her resume includes a CPA and senior roles at Arthur Andersen, Frito Lay, and Quaker Oats. Eva launched the company in a renovated sausage smokehouse in 2002 with one overriding purpose: to create enchantment through a new kind of meeting experience. Her vision was a creativity center that would have the space, staff support, and props needed to stimulate "ideation" while also delivering the highest levels of service quality.

"One Ranch goal is to always say 'yes' to our customers," says Eva. "Our staff is instructed to never tell a customer 'no.' If they are uncomfortable with 'yes,' we encourage them to say 'Give me a minute' and then find another Ranch Hand to help with an unorthodox customer request. That goal goes hand-in-hand with another—always look at a customer's experience through 'kaleidoscope eyes' to find different ways to approach an issue or request. Need an LCD projector? We have three brands to ensure compatibility with laptops. And, if that fails, a customer can borrow a jump drive and one of our computers. The best things that happen to us are customer problems; they encourage us to see customer experiences in new ways."

The Champagne Style of the Decorator

Champagne is the liquid of celebration. When people toast special occasions, more often than not it's champagne that fills their flutes. As the Rolls-Royce of beverages, it conveys a tip of the hat to excellence. It is also the favored potion of surprise and delight, the ambrosia for magical moments.

Think of Decorators as the human form of the bubbly—playful, distinctive, and a source of captivating delight. The Decorator lives to create enchanting, memorable service moments for customers. Enchanting service is different from value-added service. Ask customers what actions they would consider value-adding, and they will focus on taking an expected experience one notch higher—meaning "They gave me *more* than I anticipated." It's the upgrade, the extra helping, the complimentary dessert or the baker's dozen. Think of it as service on the upper end of a linear continuum.

Excellent service makes you smile, but enchanting service makes you swoon! As Eva Niewiadomski says, "When prospects visit Catalyst Ranch for the very first time, we do not want them to be pleasantly surprised . . . we want to take their breath away. And if a client leaves without feeling astounded and amazed, we have more work to do."

What are the secrets to creating this kind of ecstasy for customers? If Eva is the poster child for Decorator-like traits, what might we learn from her example?

Explode (Not Just Exceed) Expectations

The Decorator is always searching for opportunities to pop the cork on service experiences. The moment the cork explodes from the champagne bottle is usually an unpredictable and pleasant surprise. The Decorator seeks to evoke the same feeling of "joy unleashed" for customers.

The term Decorator is used because these Loyalty Creators decorate ordinary service experiences with acts of originality and charm. Decoration occurs when, following a manicure, the manicurist walks out to open your car door and start your engine so you won't scuff your nails. It is the housekeeper who leaves a foreign coin, flower, or kazoo on your pillow at turndown, not just a mint. It is the bank teller who opens a complimentary $5 passbook savings account on the occasion of the birth of your first child. It's the taxi driver who comps your ride because he remembers how generously you tipped him the last time he transported you.

"It's all about generosity," says Eva. "When we have a small group of six people for breakfast, two large coffee cakes would be more than enough. But we put out four or five different types. I grew up with Polish parents who taught me that the Old World way of hospitality was to make a gathering a major event. You would never skimp; you would always serve in a way that was lavish. Extra to us says you care. Two desserts at lunch confirms your manners; three creates a memory. We want our guests to remember our service as bountiful."

The Elevator Effect

Don't think of *elevator* as a quick route to the fourteenth floor; think of it as what cheerleaders do to their hometown fans! Decorators feel their charge in life is to lift the spirits of others, especially customers. They know it is the spirit of champagne that makes a moment special, not necessarily the liquid in the bottle. The magic of champagne is more in what it indicates than in how it intoxicates. In the same fashion, Decorators are not typically the glad-handing, back-slapping kind of employees. Instead of relying on hail-fellow-well-met personalities to impress customers, they seek to embellish processes, settings, and delivery systems to elevate the service mood of clients.

The Decorator takes dead aim at the intersection of service place, performance, and process to hit targets that trigger customer enchantment. Understanding that good service is a highly sensory experience, they open every sense-tickling gate in an effort to fully engage and delight customers. They are forever on the prowl for ways to take service interactions to new heights—"What if we made service prettier, enhanced by a guide, done backwards, completely tailored, designed through the eyes of a child, more effortless," and on and on. The Decorator's ideation never ceases.

"We examined every square inch of this facility to find ways to captivate," says Carrie Smith, director of operations at Catalyst Ranch. "We put make-a-sentence word magnets on the bathroom stall walls and hung dragons from the ceilings. You'll find flowers where you least expect them. You will find a colorful figurine in a total surprising place. Everything . . . I mean every single thing here . . . is a part of the creativity-enhancing experience."

Embellisher Extraordinaire
Try this. Surprise your friends by ordering a bottle of champagne the next time you go on an ordinary dinner out. It brings a touch of elegance and celebration to the event. Champagne also makes people feel more affluent than their bank accounts might suggest. The Decorator has the same

effect of making customers feel special and like their best, highest selves.

Eva Niewiadomski describes her Decorator influence on the Catalyst Ranch this way: "Some meeting facilities seek to be invisible, like the movie set people never remember. If we were a school, our goal would be to have students leave inspired, not just instructed. We partner with our customer's purpose in a way that generates pure magic. We call it 'catalyst' because the effect helps set ideas and experiences in motion. It is like what champagne does to strawberries. We want to help people who come here *become* more, not just accomplish more."

The Two Sides of the Decorator

Decorators believe in the self-fulfilling principle that if you expect the best and demonstrate the best, you almost always get back the best in return. They teach others that distinctive service doesn't require a complex formula but is accomplished by understanding customer expectations and then going them one—or two—better.

Of course, while the give-more-than-you-get philosophy is the very soul of great service, when taken to extremes it can lead to a quick trip to the poor house.

The best Decorators learn to embellish and amend in areas that have the biggest impact on customer loyalty, redirecting time or resources away from those performance dimensions that have little effect on customers' repurchase intentions. You have only to make a special request or encounter an inconvenience at the Catalyst Ranch to witness their Decorators springing rapidly into action to not only answer your request but ensure you are well taken care of.

We were facilitating a meeting at the Catalyst Ranch and could not get the temperature in the meeting room to a comfortable level. Unlike most meeting facilities, at Catalyst Ranch the customer has complete control over the heating and air conditioning. We quickly found Elizabeth, who returned to the meeting room to determine the cause of the problem. Unable to figure out a solution, she quickly summoned an operations manager. The operations manager apologized for the inconvenience and explained that this room had two ventilation systems and that one of the controls had been inadvertently hidden from view behind a large piece of furniture. She provided instructions on how best to adjust the temperature to us as well as to Elizabeth, who was embarrassed that she had not known about the "secret controls." For the next two days, Elizabeth paid several visits to our meeting room to ensure the "secret controls" were functioning appropriately. No matter which staff member we encountered over the two days, they stopped to inquire if the "secret controls" were functioning properly. The "secret controls" approach by the staff was obviously an embellishment of what could have become a less-than-pleasant memory. They turned the situation into a fun memory at their great meeting facility.

Leading the Decorator

Decorators are among the rarest of Loyalty Creators. In a crowd of fifty servers, you might be lucky to find one natural-born Decorator. But there is no shortage of Decorator wannabes who, with the right care and feeding, can blossom into the real thing.

There is a tendency to think Decorators have flamboyant, quirky personalities, but the truth is they are often understated and business-like. Their power lies less in sheer force of personality than in an abiding inventiveness and capacity to grasp what out-of-the-ordinary experiences and special touches will delight their customers.

Create Supportive Cultures

Magical service flourishes amid supportive and caring cultures. One of the first things you notice about the employees of Catalyst Ranch is their teamwork and liberal recognition of others' efforts. "Let me help with that" and "Girl, you are really good" sprinkle their behind-the-scenes dialogue. Catalyst employees act as if they get just as much joy out of helping each other look good as they do in helping the customer feel good. That kind of behavior takes its cues and cascades down from the leadership of an organization.

Affirm Others

Affirming efforts to deliver memorable service is one of the best ways to produce more of the same kind of behavior. Employees at Catalyst Ranch hold frequent gatherings to brainstorm ideas for boosting customer service, and those who come up with the best ideas—or who are caught in the act of exceeding customer expectations—are celebrated for their performance. If a clever idea fails or backfires, Ranch leaders spend more time helping associates extract lessons from the experience than assigning blame.

LEADING THE DECORATOR

Insist on kindness to others.

Be quick to provide affirmation.

Remind employees of the service vision in word and deed.

Encourage employees to get on the high wire (take risks).

Be the net that catches employees when they fall off the wire.

Be crystal clear about the limits of freedom.

Be your employees' greatest fan.

Ask a Catalyst Ranch leader how he or she affirms people who deliver exemplary service, and you'll likely hear a long, diverse list of recognition practices. One of the best affirmation tactics in our eyes is how customers are involved in recognition efforts. A customer comment about a delicious snack, for example, might lead to a response like, "That's the specialty of our snack pros—Lauren and Caroline," with the praise being communicated directly to the employees or even broadcast throughout the company. As operations manager Rob Hanlin puts it, "Praise for Ranch Hands from our customers is more important than praise from one of the managers. It reminds them of who they are here for."

Cover the Basics First

Customers value the extras only after their basic needs are met. They won't be impressed by the complimentary newspaper or free Wi-Fi access if the heating or cooling system in their hotel room malfunctions. The personable flight attendant and tasty meal in an upgraded first-class seat vanishes from memory when the plane lands too late to make a critical connection. Customers only love Catalyst Ranch *after* the commode flushes, the meeting room chairs feel comfortable, all needed supplies are on hand, and the air conditioning works.

"We are about courtesy and creativity. That is what our customers see," says Eva. "But behind the scenes we are all about efficiency and taking care of the basics. There are things that are fundamental to good hospitality and employees are not allowed to ignore them. We encourage our people to dress artistically, but we also require them to dress professionally. We would never hire someone our corporate customers could not accept."

Empowering the Decorator

"It is hard to change the paradigm from within the paradigm," wrote Albert Einstein. The kind of service experiences that leave customers shaking their heads with surprise and delight emerge from outside the usual service paradigm. Such innovation takes daring and valor.

The role of the service leader is to nurture that kind of courage, even when the leader is unable to reasonably predict its outcome. Says Eva, "If you believe in your employees and want them to try new things, you encourage them to do so not just through words but through actions. When two of our people, Lauren and Caroline, mentioned we should do something special with our snacks, I realized they had a passion for desserts. We funded their snack R&D effort and it yielded tremendous results. We now have a snack manual with hundreds of ideas. Our customers not only rave about our snacks, they rave about our two snack pros!"

Decorators are architects of uncommon service experiences, the kind of encounters that build lasting memories and make customers thirst for repeat performances. Like that cherished bottle of champagne, they make customers feel as if they are "tasting stars." And in today's world of bland, indifferent customer service, there is no better way to set you apart from the masses.

6

The Conscience

"Rather fail with honor than succeed by fraud."

—SOPHOCLES

Honor and trust are the lifeblood of repeat business. To serve well is to enter into a covenant with customers—one that promises that the customers' best interests will be taken to heart. When customers suspect disrespect or deceit on the part of service providers—a deficit of honor—the odds that they will grace your doorstep again fall precipitously.

What does the word "honor" really imply? The dictionary tells us it is "nobility of soul and a scorn of meanness." The word also suggests a state of discipline, courage, and honesty. Honor is the soul of the service covenant. We rely on it to govern fair and proper practice.

Service interactions aren't regulated by formal contracts that bind the server and the served to virtuous behaviors—customers simply assume they'll be treated in a respectful, ethical, and civil manner. When they aren't, cracks begin to form in the relationship. Should customers experience further disrespectful or dishonest behavior, those fissures grow into fault lines that permanently sever the relationship.

The Loyalty Creator we call the Conscience is the sentinel of customer trust. The Conscience does more than model service with honor; he reminds others of their covenant with customers. The Conscience reminds leaders and colleagues of the power of service ethics. The Conscience knows that dealing fairly and honestly with customers is not only the right thing to do, it is also one of the best ways to create the kind of devoted customers that add dollars to the bottom line.

Profiling the Conscience

The Conscience is the embodiment of honor and trusted action. We were staying at the Embassy Suites and decided to ask the hotel staff for a restaurant recommendation. "Do you like seafood?" front-desk clerk Jessica Paskiewicz inquired. When we said we did, she enthusiastically recommended an upscale seafood restaurant. "Let me call them right now and get you a great table." This was behavior you might expect of a concierge at a luxury hotel, not a front desk employee at a more modestly priced property.

The restaurant provided us a delightful experience with attentive service. When we declined dessert after a delicious meal, the waiter brought to our table a plate of small cookies and hearty strawberries. "These are compliments of Jessica," he proudly announced. We were blown away. How did this happen? We had to know more about what made Jessica tick, and what kind of service system produced this kind of above-and-beyond behavior.

Returning to the hotel front desk, we queried Jessica about the process. "Well," she said, "we get terrific reviews on that restaurant or I would not send my guests there. And they are very kind to all of us at the hotel. Sometimes I get an envelope with $20 in it. It never says where it came from, or what it is about, but I am pretty sure it is their way of thanking us for the referrals." Instead of making us flinch, Jessica's openness and honesty actually raised our trust levels. She didn't attempt to hide anything, nor did she portray her behavior as strictly saintly. The result was that the hotel won, we won . . . and best of all, Jessica won!

We say "Scout's honor" to pledge our absolute *honesty.* Honor in service situations requires complete truthfulness—the truth, the whole truth, and nothing but the truth. We trust service providers when, after making an error, they "own" their infraction by apologizing and being straightforward rather than evasive or deceitful. While we might be disappointed in an outcome, we respect service workers who don't lean on excuses, point fingers elsewhere, say they were "only following policy," or give us lengthy, tortured explanations for problems.

Nothing builds bonds with customers like feelings of trust. When they believe organizations have their best interests at heart, and when they are consistently treated with a sense of fairness and respect, they'll stick to your company like Super Glue.

Courage Under Fire

Customer trust is so important to the Conscience that he will exercise valor to ensure it. This boldness often manifests as "empowerment through conviction." Customers like dealing with someone who has the authority to solve their problems or answer their questions on the spot; research shows the ability to resolve customer issues on first contact is one of the best ways to win their confidence and continued loyalty. Customers also believe the attitude of the entire organization is reflected in the authority given the front line. If they deal with employees who don't seem to be trusted by the organization, they assume they will be treated the same.

The Tattered Cover in Denver is one of the largest independent bookstores in America. The bookstore came under attack when owner Joyce Meskis refused to release the book-purchasing records of a customer who was part of a criminal investigation. Losing her case in the lower courts, Meskis funded an expensive appeal on the grounds of her customers' First Amendment rights. Not only did she win the case, she won the admiration of consumers around the world. Even those who disagreed with her position praised her courage in the face of strong opposition and risk of significant financial loss. Meskis is the Conscience personified.

Guardians of Trust

As the chief customer "trustodian," the Conscience knows trust must be maintained at all times—even one slip-up can cause customers to question an organization's motives and unravel a hard-won bond. This Loyalty Creating trait requires staying vigilant and dedicated to finding weak spots in the organization's trust-building efforts. Like a mother who uses any means necessary to protect a child in danger, the Conscience doesn't blindly follow company policy, practice, or protocol when trust is in jeopardy. When these Loyalty Creators come across a customer complaint that represents a violation of the customer's best interests, they take immediate action to ensure the situation doesn't escalate and that trust is restored.

John Gutweniger, an assistant manager in the call center of AIG Insurance in Lake Mary, Florida, was nearing the end of a long shift when a supervisor called to say an irate customer was demanding to speak to a manager. No sooner had John greeted the customer than the blistering began. "She was hysterical, her words a combination of screams and sobs," John says. "She had just purchased an auto insurance policy through our sales department earlier that day. Being that she was on an extremely limited budget, she asked that her down payment be deducted from her account the following day (Friday) when she got paid. She claimed that this was agreed to. However, she found out otherwise when she tried to purchase groceries later that evening and was told the account was overdrawn." The customer demanded her money be refunded immediately and her policy cancelled; John knew there was no way for him to refund her money that night and attempted to explain this as gently as possible. "What followed was about fifteen minutes of screaming about the fact that she was a single mother with two children living from paycheck to paycheck," John says. "She informed me she had no food at home for her children other than moldy bread. I was speechless."

Not knowing how to respond, John asked the only question that came to mind: "Other than getting your refund back to you tonight, is there anything at all I can do for you?" She paused for a moment and said sarcastically, "Yeah, you can buy us dinner."

"Of course," John said. "Why hadn't I thought of that?" I asked her if her children liked pizza. Somewhat confused, she responded that they did. I asked her if she would allow me to have a pizza sent to her house that evening. She initially declined; however, I insisted. Finally, she accepted my offer."

John went online, found a Pizza Hut in her town, and had a large pepperoni pizza along with an order of cinnamon bread sent to her house. Driving home that night, he felt a sense of peace about himself. "Although I knew the customer would certainly be canceling her policy as soon as her refund was processed, it wasn't about her business any more; it was about her welfare as a human being." Once the refund was processed, John—ever the Conscience—contacted the woman one more time to apologize for everything that had happened. He said he was sorry to lose her as a customer and informed her if she ever decided to come back to contact him directly. "She informed me that she would not be coming back. I wished her the best and prepared to close the call."

"One other thing," she stated. "Yes?" I replied. "Thank you for the pizza."

Living the "Us" in Trust

Living the "us" in trust involves remembering that trust is not one-sided; it is an exchange between two individuals. It is not something that happens by accident. Instead, trust must be crafted "by hand." Trust can only be built over time, through a series of consistent and congruent actions that convey reliability and credibility.

The magic of trust is that it quickly compounds—show trust to customers, and they'll trust you back. Customers who trust you, and feel trusted in return, typically buy more, forgive your mistakes, frequently return, and refer you.

Waiters at Vincenzo's Ristorante in Omaha, Nebraska, greet patrons at their tables with a pitcher of "honor wine"— a high-end Chianti. "Enjoy this if you like," a waitress told a group of us one night. "We charge by the glass. At the end of the meal just let me know how many glasses you had and I'll add it to your bill." It is a powerful opening gesture of trust. When I asked the restaurant owner on our way out how many patrons drank the "honor wine" and accurately reported what they consumed, he smiled and said, "Most do . . . it's one of our best features!" The restaurant has twice been voted "Best of Omaha" by *Omaha City Weekly*.

Pros and Cons of the Conscience

The Conscience employee demonstrates a decency that reminds people to do the right thing. But the exemplars also take care to avoid a "mother knows best" attitude. On the contrary, they understand people are fallible and are often tempted to cut corners or make decisions that, because of organizational policies or peer pressure, don't always have customers' best interests in mind. The Conscience leads not by pontificating from a soapbox but by taking personal actions that regularly put principle before profit.

Because of the Conscience's high standards, he often needles people about putting more passion in their service efforts or doing more to exceed, not just meet, customer expectations. To employees looking to do just the minimum to get by, Consciences can seem self-righteous and annoying.

To leaders sensitive to the chain of command, this sometimes-overbearing behavior can feel out of line or even threatening. Less confident leaders who attempt to tone down the high-minded behavior, telling the Conscience to "relax a little" or that "everyone slacks off at times," can trigger rebellion. Some managers even look for ways to marginalize the impact and influence of the Conscience. They often lose a great and important resource in the process.

How to Lead the Conscience

The Conscience thrives in environments where a premium is placed on trust. These are cultures where leaders regularly demonstrate faith in colleagues and subordinates and are trusted themselves due to the consistency of their words and actions.

Be Humble, But Strong

"Trust," according to *Pioneering Organizations* author Larry Davis, is defined as "a state of readiness for unguarded interaction with someone or thing." We lower our human shields only if the intentions of those we're interacting with are perceived as integrity-based or if their competence is highly valued. In other words, we trust two classes of people: those whom we believe are not out to do us in, and those we perceive have the capacity to do what we trust them to do.

Trust is also a function of vulnerability, or of not being afraid to show others your weaknesses as well as strengths. But be cautioned. While some humility is a virtue, too much humbleness or self-deprecation can undermine the confidence of followers in their leaders. Be humble and transparent—but not at the expense of looking less than authoritative.

The Power of Congruence

Congruence means that your actions and behaviors are in harmony with your words. Andy DiSabatino, CEO of Wilmington, Delaware–based EDiS Corporation, a construction and property management company, puts it this way: "You can tell a lot about a leader by the way he or she treats a carpenter or a bulldozer operator." Leaders engender trust when their actions behind closed doors match what the public witnesses, when their beliefs don't change with prevailing winds, and, most importantly, when they support their people in tough times.

Leaders who are trusted take time to investigate, rather than rush to judgment, when customers charge their employees with rude or incompetent service. They know that publicly upbraiding their people to appease customers—without first seeking evidence of wrongdoing—can undermine trust among front-line employees for years to come.

Congruent leaders provide the Conscience with a sense of security. When employees know that their quest for ethical and moral behaviors will be supported—if not always understood—they are more confident in asserting their values. They are more apt to give their all if managed by leaders who regularly seek to strike a balance between the best interests of the customer and of the organization, rather than leaning too heavily to the latter.

LEADING THE CONSCIENCE EMPLOYEE

Be the attitude you want to see in others.

Express clear gratitude for the role, not just the results.

Communicate optimism and a firm belief in a positive outcome.

Help people appreciate the nobility of their contributions.

Be clear about your expectations for excellence.

Believe in the greatness of others.

Never accept mediocrity when the capacity of greatness is present.

Lead with Courage

It's a truism that the business world often sacrifices principles on the altar of profits. Shady dealings are justified in the name of competitiveness, corners are cut to meet quarterly revenue and profit goals, and "need to know" policies and "for your eyes only" files can sometimes telegraph a deficit of ethics or honor.

A recent study done by ABC News and reported in *USA Today* asked this question: "If a manager is discovered to have engaged in unethical behavior that results primarily in corporate gain, should he/she be reprimanded?" While a predictable 13 percent of greedy Gordon Gekko–types answered "no," a surprising 36 percent of those interviewed said they were "not sure."

Against that backdrop, the Conscience must often buck the tide and assume a less-than-popular position. Advocating for the client can put the Conscience at odds with the crowd that is eager to run roughshod over the customer, as well as those who are willing to risk poor word of mouth and repeat business for short-term organizational gain. But the Conscience doesn't feel so alone when supported by leaders who show an equal amount of gumption.

In his monthly column on strategy in the October 2002 issue of *Fast Company* magazine, John Ellis wrote, "Here's what real business leaders do. They go out and rally the troops, plant the flag, and make a stand. They confront hostile audiences and they deal with the press. If the issue is confidence, they conduct themselves confidently. If the issue is trust, they make their company's business transparent. If the issue is character, they tell the truth. They do not shirk responsibility; they assume command. Because a fundamental ingredient of business success is leadership. And the granular stuff of leadership is courage, conviction, and character."

Honor is the fundamental expression of civility and consideration—that is, people behaving as they should toward other people. Shakespeare has Antony tell Octavia before the battle with Augustus, "If I lose my honor, I lose myself." So it is with the Conscience, who feels if he fails the customer, he fails everything his organization should stand for.

7 The Giver

"The smallest good deed is better
than the grandest good intention."

—JOSEPH DUQUET

Give the very best that you have, and the best will come back to you. It's a philosophy many of us are taught as children. It's also the attitude that shapes service-centered Boy or Girl Scouts, produces philanthropic leaders, and informs how many people approach their jobs each day. It's also an axiom with a promise of reciprocity: "the best will come back to you." Some might interpret it as meaning, "Those with good fortune deserve what they get because they have made contributions of similar size to the world."

But the variety of Loyalty Creator we call the Giver doesn't seek tit for tat. What makes Givers distinctive—and what helps them turn indifferent or skeptical customers into passionately loyal ones—is a belief that the simple act of giving brings its own rewards.

The Giver is all about grace. Grace is the word we use to characterize athletes who perform effortlessly, manners that reveal refinement, and others who exude class. However, the most profound definition of grace is "undeserved love." It means pure affection—that is, affinity without reason or expectation. The Giver serves with grace, not because customers have earned such attention but because all fellow human beings are worthy of respect and care.

What's important to know about Givers is that their propensity to give emanates from an almost unconditional belief in the goodness of others. As one senior executive told us in describing a Giver on her front-line staff, "He can take the super livid customers that others label as 'crazy' and simply love them back to sanity. You can actually watch the transformation. He simply refuses to give up on bringing out the goodness from the surliest customers. . . . And it almost always works."

We like to think of the Giver's approach as "grandmother-style service." Grandmothers spoil you just because they get a kick out of it, remember your favorite everything, always give you a little bit extra, and cheer you up when others chastise. Givers are the service equivalent of customers' grandmas.

The Giver's Cornucopia

Givers have several sides to their benevolent personalities. Think of them as human cornucopias, that conical shell filled with a bounty of great things that is often used as a symbol for Thanksgiving.

We have had the good fortune of being served by every variety of this gifting person. Without exception, they leave an array of blessings and positive memories in their path. Gandhi challenged us to "be the change you would wish for the world." The Giver works to "be the positive energy that lights up the world." Following are four ways that the Giver spirit takes shape and helps to "Velcro" customers to your organization.

The Bighearted Celebrator

Walk into the lobby of Hamburger University at McDonald's Corporation's world headquarters in Oak Brook, Illinois, and you find an environment that oozes the company's culture. The large stone building sits on the banks of a lazy lake. An exact reconstruction of founder Ray Kroc's office sits in one corner, complete with his favorite piano. The expansive use of glass draws in warmth from the outside while inside it reflects the eagerness of new managers present for training.

At the center of this welcoming scene is party host and "happiness choreographer" Dave Spion. His mile-wide smile and animated manner suggest the bearing of a concierge or greeter rather than the security guard that Dave is. "Oh, no," he announces to everyone within earshot, "they let you guys come back. Who do I need call and warn?" he jokes. Employees passing through the lobby shake their heads and smile, amazed and fortified by Dave's relentless enthusiasm.

You can't get to the visitor sign-in log without passing through Dave's cordial handshake. "You don't have to use your real name," he teases and winks, keeping the fun machine revved up. All the leg-pulling entertainment is only an appetizer for the abundant service entrée about to be delivered. Attentive and anticipatory, Dave engulfs guests with a smorgasbord of big-hearted gestures:

"You can leave your luggage back here with me."

"Let me know when you plan to leave and I can get you a taxi."

"The hot coffee is up the steps and to your right, and it's well worth the short walk."

"She is not answering her phone, so let me call the person in the next office to see if he knows where she is."

If Dave Spion were a grandmother, he'd make sure you got your favorite dessert, were tucked in tight, and he'd leave the light on in the hall so you'd feel safe. But don't think for a minute that this makes Dave a pushover as a security guard. No one gets past the security desk without following all the proper procedures, and Dave is constantly on the prowl for anything that looks suspicious or unusual in the environment. Yet through his giving spirit and big-hearted practices, he makes every customer and employee feel prized, not policed.

TLC Squared

When someone suggests adding a little TLC (tender loving care) to a service encounter, they are usually attempting to turn gloom into glad. One of the master TLC-givers we know is Daryl Roe. Daryl is the executive assistant to several executives with General Growth Properties (GGP) in downtown Chicago. GGP is the country's largest owner and manager of regional malls. As part of a company committed to great service—for consumers, retailers, owners, and employees—Daryl is the embodiment of the service attitude the company aspires to consistently deliver.

"Let me give you a Daryl story," says GGP executive vice president Jean Schlemmer. "We decided to move my office to a different location on the same floor. I turned it over to Daryl and went on a long overdue vacation. When I came back, she had done way more than move me. She had decorated my office—and in my favorite colors. She had a caricature of me that had appeared in our new annual report matted and framed. Remembering I was a cat person, she bought a couple of Garfield-like statuettes for my bookcase. I could go on and on. I told her she had gone way beyond the call of duty but Daryl does everything like that. She remembers the personal details and finds a way to incorporate them in her special brand of service philanthropy. I have had assistants who added value. I have had assistants who added efficiency. I have never had an assistant so great at adding *love*."

TLC-squared employees do sometimes need gentle reminding when their affection and giving ways start to border on smothering behavior. Your grandmother probably had the same challenge. "But wouldn't it be great," says GGP CEO John Bucksbaum, "if we faced the glorious challenge of having to tone down all of our employees because they gave too much!"

The Philanthropist

Tree trimming is among the toughest of occupations. Imagine being perched at the very top of a giant oak, supported only by pulleys and ropes while operating a bulky, powerful chain saw. These arbor aerialists not only risk falling from great heights, they hazard getting hit by falling limbs.

Tree trimmers aren't typically noted for their service sensitivity, but tree surgeon Richard Butler is clearly an exception. Butler's Tree Service is located near Gun Barrel, Texas. It has long served as caretaker for the massive oak trees on Chip's two-acre yard on Cedar Creek Lake. Richard's service approach is as impressive as his team's Cirque du Soleil antics in tall trees. For example, realizing one of his customers was an author, Richard requested a signed copy of "the latest book" as a part of his payment.

Not long ago Chip needed to have a dozen tree stumps ground out of his yard and asked Richard for an estimate. Satisfied with the price, work began a few days later. But further examination of the terrain revealed three stumps that were previous overlooked. "If you could please give me another copy of your book, *Beep Beep!*" Richard announced, "I'll throw these stumps in at no extra charge."

On another occasion, the Bells had lightning strike a large elm tree on the property. A call was placed to Richard to "come out and give us an estimate." Upon arriving home after work, the Bells found the tree gone and the stump removed. On the back door was not an invoice. It was Richard's business card. On the back of his card were four words written in the language of service givers: "No charge. Beep Beep!"

Random Acts of Kindness

Givers can enliven the sometimes monotonous banter of everyday service interactions. We know Dave will always delight guests with his unique service stage management. We can count on Daryl's above-and-beyond attention. We can depend on Richard's special charity. But there is another type of Giver whose stock in trade is surprise.

Sherri Schafer is a "random acts of kindness" specialist. A customer experience professional at Southern California Edison (SCE) based in Rosemead, California, Sherri delights in surprising customers and colleagues with unexpected gestures—simply for the feeling of joy it creates. She never forgets a birthday or special occasion. And she adorns every act of kindness with plenty of "sparkly."

A few days after Chip spoke at one of SCE's "customer hero" celebrations, he got a special present in the mail. It was a tiny cartoon character figurine of a speaker at a lectern. But Sherri went one step further. She cut out and pasted a Texas hat and Texas star on the figure, and covered the lectern with an exact replica of the Chip Bell Group logo—the precise colors and fonts.

"Sherri is an extraordinarily giving person and this comes out in a myriad of ways," says SCE manager Stephen Scott. Scott relates this example of Sherri's giving spirit: "The SCE call center has in the past helped the company organize activities for national customer service week. However, this year because of the increased call volume, mandatory overtime, and being over budget, the call center pulled back its activities during the week, which is historically a morale booster for the call center reps. But Sherri wanted to let the customer service representatives know how important they were to the organization, so she recruited volunteers from outside of the call center to bake homemade cookies for each rep."

How to Lead a Giver

Many people talk about making a difference, but Givers turn the talk into action every day. For customers or colleagues on the receiving end of their generosity, Givers' big-heartedness can literally make a day and renew faith in the human race. Watch Dave, Sherri, Richard, or Daryl in action and you find yourself thinking, "Why can't human relationships always be like that?"

Lest you think that Givers are without flaw, know that their generous spirit can sometimes have drawbacks. For one, they can get overextended and risk burnout if they get caught up in the "disease to please." They are often the last to ask for assistance, fearing they will let someone down. That means their giving nature needs to be monitored.

When Hurricane Hugo passed through Charlotte, North Carolina, in 1989, plenty of Givers went into overdrive. There's a famous story of a Duke Energy Company lineman who fell asleep behind the wheel at a green traffic light. Most drivers who came up behind the Duke truck quickly figured out the situation and quietly drove around the vehicle, letting the weary lineman—no doubt a Giver extraordinaire—catch a few extra winks.

Shepherding the Giver

The symbolism of the shepherd is particularly appropriate for managing Givers because they need protection more than they do direction. Getting Givers motivated is rarely a problem; getting them to slow down or take a breath is a different issue altogether. Rather than protecting Givers from others, the bigger challenge for the leader is, in essence, to protect the Giver from herself.

While in an ideal world all who need help would receive it, the Giver needs to learn to pick her battles and periodically stop for rest and recharging. Trying to be a hero all the time is a ticket to burnout, and without self-regulation Givers can easily crash or find themselves so overextended their performance begins to suffer.

The Leader As Agent

Givers also need leaders who act as agents of a sort. Not to help them seek more fame or fortune, but to run interference through advocating, explaining, and defending. Consider the agent for an extraordinarily talented but outrageously eccentric stage performer. Such an agent makes sure the stage is set to ensure success. If some critic or cynic communicates doubt or raises eyebrows following an absurd request by the performer, the agent doesn't question or reproach her client. The agent simply explains or repeats the request with the resolve of an athletic coach asking a trainer for some extra towels. Leaders of Givers need to show the same sense of sponsorship and loyalty.

The Giver Loyalty Creator isn't like the rest of us. She not only sees the world differently, her special perspective leads her to take unique, extreme, or even excessive routes to creating caring experiences for customers and colleagues. That sometimes will lead to judgment or mocking behavior from coworkers, who may accuse the Giver of grandstanding or even brownnosing.

What do great service leaders do in such situations? They agent! It is not that managers fail to see the eccentricity in Givers' actions. They simply see the behavior as a special gift, with benefits that far outweigh drawbacks. These leaders stand firm in their advocacy and are unfailing in their support of Givers.

The Leader As Camp Counselor

The best camp counselors have a way of enabling fun and instilling discipline at the same time. Their playful spirits create joyful and entertaining activities, but they aren't afraid to rein kids in if their antics overstep camp etiquette. They are able to bridle without binding, control without oppressing.

So it is with leaders who are skilled at managing Givers. When GGP executive Jean Schlemmer has had to tell Daryl Roe that her generosity is bordering on excessive, she's done it in a way that is direct but not directive, assertive but not critical. "Daryl welcomes feedback," says Schlemmer. "And if you are too subtle, she quickly reads that there is probably more feedback you are not giving. . . . Candor works. Compassion works. Indirectness does not."

LEADING THE GIVER

Don't let the humility of the Giver restrain your affirmation.

Look for ways the distinctive gifts of the Giver can have their most profound influence in your organization.

Lace your relationship with total authenticity. Givers see you as you are, not as you pretend to be.

Grant Givers the space to be demonstrative; they cannot help it.

Provide Givers with candid feedback when the burdens of their generosity exceed its benefits.

Help others see the virtues of the spirit of the Giver.

The Leader As Guardian

Givers are often easy targets for those seeking to undermine their impact and special contributions. Some coworkers, perhaps fearing they'll appear selfish or lackadaisical by comparison, see Givers as "blowing the curve" when managers rate individuals on their teamwork skills or making extra efforts to help customers. That often leads to backhanded comments about the Giver.

Such gossip can ruin the reputation of employees who should be emulated, and it dims the light that shines in Givers. It calls for leaders courageous enough to call the game and who let people know that they'll be held accountable for such derisive behavior.

Try this test. Apply your own brand of the Dave-Daryl-Richard-Sherri giving spirit for thirty days. Give abundantly—to customers or coworkers—without any expectation of return or even appreciation. Then take measure of how you feel at the end of that month. We're betting you'll feel so buoyant and gratified you'll want to try it again. And that your customers will tell you they were on the receiving end of some of the best, most selfless service they've experienced in some time.

PART TWO

LEADING YOUR LOYALTY CREATORS

Remarkable service can occur without great leadership. All organizations have associates who work to give great service simply out of the belief that customers deserve their best efforts. But to ensure that distinctive service happens consistently across an organization, and in a manner that supports a company's service vision, skilled, authentic, and passionate leaders are required.

The behavior and practices of leaders can cause the spirit to serve to be embraced or resisted; held in esteem or rebuked as a frill; supported or ignored. Leaders who nurture Loyalty Creators need not be charismatic and charming to be effective. They must, however, be clear and sincere about the priority they place on serving customers well. They must be persistent in ensuring service quality doesn't get lost amid other organizational objectives, and they must be committed to finding time amid busy schedules to coach, mentor, and support Loyalty Creators on the front lines.

Leadership is the thrust of this second part of the book. Leadership, in our view, has little to do with being a manager, supervisor, or boss—in other words, with positional power. Great leadership can come from the security guard who alerts a plant manager that a departing, seemingly happy customer had disparaging words as he left the facility. It can come from the gate attendant who suggests that snacks be taken from a grounded plane to serve weary passengers holed up in a waiting area because of a weather delay. Or it can come from a battle-worn nurse who privately but sternly asserts her concern for a patient's welfare to a too-busy-to-listen physician.

Effective leaders of Loyalty Creators connect, involve, inspire, support, and encourage. They are the keepers of organizational values and perpetuators of standards of excellence. Leaders don't make great service happen. But they do play a vital role in creating the conditions and providing the support that enables others to serve to the best of their ability every day.

The Roles of the Service Leader

There are seven traits or actions we've identified in our research that differentiate exemplary service leaders from their less-successful counterparts, represented in the following figure.

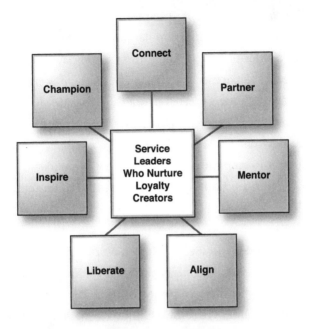

Connect

Trace the origin of the word "rapport," and you will discover that it is related to the concept of kinship. Kinship is the experience associates get from leaders who lead with *realness,* not *role-ness.* When a leader shows authenticity, sincere curiosity, and appropriate vulnerability, it causes employees to lower their defenses and relate with openness. Good leader-associate connections pave the way for effective and enduring employee-customer connections.

Partner

"Leader as servant" is a popular phrase that suggests leaders should dismount the high horse of power. We believe that "leader as partner" can be an even more powerful concept. Partner leaders create relationships that are vision-centered, not power-centered. Partner leaders focus on support, not subservience; on commitment, not compliance. Partner leaders enlist employees as fellow alliance builders, working as equals for the greater good of creating loyal customers.

Mentor

One of the greatest gifts one person can give another is the gift of wisdom and support. When leaders function as mentors, they nurture employee confidence through competence and employee resourcefulness through knowledge. Mentor leaders understand the hard-won lessons and advice they pass on to employees gets "paid forward" when those same employees mentor customers—and eventually other coworkers. The more customers grow at the hand of a server, the more cemented their loyalty becomes.

Align

Customer trust is built by consistently delivering on promises. When the customer's experience matches what the organization promises or implies through advertising, prior service experiences, or word of mouth, the customer comes to rely on service providers as trustworthy. To achieve such an end, leaders must ensure that what an organization promises and what it delivers are aligned and consistent from location to location—and from server to server.

Liberate

Empowerment does not translate to *unlimited license* but rather *responsible freedom.* Effective leaders give Loyalty Creators the freedom to solve customer problems and answer questions on the spot *within flexible guidelines.* Customers use the level of front-line empowerment as a peephole into the values of an organization. The more they witness or experience employees who act with authority on their behalf, the more their confidence in the organization soars.

Inspire

Leaders who inspire spur creativity and productivity among their associates. A major study done on the most productive research and development units in the world—those with the most patents and the most profound breakthroughs—found their employees labeled their R&D leaders as inspiring. They did not mean their leaders had charisma or charm. Rather, they pointed to leaders' willingness to be bold in their decisions, courageous in their support, and ethical in their nature. Inspirational leaders cultivate pioneers—employees who think imaginatively in their quest to give customers one-of-a-kind experiences and plenty of stories to tell.

Champion

Leaders who champion are quick to affirm and slow to critique. They know that the greatest need of human beings is to feel valued. And they constantly seek the means, moments, and methods to convey gratitude and encouragement for service greatness. Leaders who champion also grasp an important truth: Servers who feel affirmed and appreciated are more likely to elicit those same feelings in the customers they serve.

Connect

"It's better to be a lion for a day than
a sheep all your life."

—SISTER ELIZABETH KENNY

Hundreds of employees poured into the giant hotel ballroom. Room lights dimmed as the spotlights bathed the massive stage and accentuated its colorful, themed background. The sound tech's voice boomed over the speaker system: "Ladies and gentlemen, the CEO of Acme Manufacturing, Jack Topdog."

The CEO, carefully scripted through a teleprompter and supported by dazzling slides, detailed the financial history of the company and its projected goals. The scene was a carbon copy of a gazillion other big-deal meetings held in hundreds of ballrooms around the world. But this one was different in one important way.

Without warning, the CEO moved beyond the teleprompter to the edge of the stage, signaling a change in tone from pragmatism to passion. As the CEO began to talk about the power of the company's vision and the value of every employee in bringing it to fruition, tears began to fall to the stage floor. His overflowing emotion necessitated several long pauses to regain composure. As the CEO's speech concluded, there was a long silence. The audience sat stunned by what it had just witnessed. Then they leapt to their feet for a long standing ovation. Even the "way too serious" sound technicians were on their feet!

It was not the tears that moved this audience. It was the CEO's courage to be unabashedly authentic—to be publicly real, regardless of how others might view his actions. Whether the emotion displayed is anger, compassion, pain, or joy, leaders who are authentic create a more powerful connection with their employees, one that builds a higher level of trust and support. And when the going gets tough—when customers are complaining, overtime is required, or budgets are being slashed—it's that connection that keeps followers firmly behind their leaders.

Leaders too often associate their mantle of authority with a requirement for detachment. "I don't care if my employees like me," you will often hear managers proclaim, "I just want them to respect me." Such a view is often a preamble to emotional distance. Aloofness as the expression of authority invites employee indifference and evasiveness—a tendency to evade the truth or to cover up problems—not enthusiasm or honesty. An open-door policy is not about a piece of furniture. It is about communicating to employees that they can be open and real with you without fear of recrimination or judgment.

Organizations with an abundance of authentic leaders often feature high levels of employee engagement and strong track records of product and service innovation. Turnover tends to be lower because employees value environments free of passive-aggressive game playing, finger-pointing, and posturing by leaders. Customers often stay in the fold longer because they trust what they experience. Suppliers typically give such organizations better breaks because dealing with leaders they can trust leads to long-term relationships, not one-time transactions.

Leaders Who Connect Don't Wear Rank

During combat, military leaders remove the markings of their rank while in the field. This is done so they cannot be easily identified and targeted by enemy snipers. However, as an infantry unit commander in Viet Nam, Chip often observed that this perceived flattening of hierarchy also took the focus off of "whom" and placed it squarely on "what"— accomplishing the mission successfully as a cohesive unit.

We had invited a fellow consultant to assist us in working with the executive team of a long-term client. She had heard us repeatedly rave about the CEO of this high-tech company. Her flight was delayed, and the meeting was under way when she arrived, preventing us from introducing her to the audience. After listening to the group engage in a lengthy, spirited dialogue over a strategic challenge, she whispered to one of us, "Which one is the CEO?" It was the highest compliment that leader, who was fond of saying, "Never add any more leadership than is needed," could have received.

Leaders unconcerned with rank and power busy themselves with the business of mission and course, not might and conceit. The result is usually happier employees, happier customers—and a healthier bottom line.

Loyalty Creator Leaders Care About Spirit

"This is the best work I have ever done in my life," said a colleague who had just completed a very difficult consulting project. Although there was pride in his voice, even more apparent was the lump in his throat and the emotion in his eyes. Chores extract toil, but causes unearth enthusiasm. Real leaders care as much about the expression of the passion as the quality of the toil. They do this by constantly reminding people of the cause—"the joy of delighting customers and building repeat business"—and by demonstrating their own passion for that mission.

Animation Invites Passion

"You *are* Interstate Hotels and Resorts," said Vice President Jill Kallmeyer at a recent all-managers conference. "So take personally every encounter with every guest and every associate." The words come from a woman renowned for her passion for employees and customers and her "I'm so excited" presence. Standout service leaders look for ways to connect and add value to every encounter with coworkers or clients. Instead of learning about customer experiences from a static survey, they find out face-to-face and ear-to-ear. They are "myth-averse," preferring to unearth the facts rather than rely on hearsay or innuendo. And their up close and personal approach usually builds passionate followers.

"There is more to 'turning lemons into lemonade' than just positive thinking," says Dallas-based motivational speaker Ed Foreman. "Lemons take very little energy, but lemonade is a creation you have to work at." When Foreman was scheduled to do an all-day workshop at an invitation-only event in Scotland, he arrived to learn the sponsor had been unable to enlist a single participant for his session. "Don't worry," the sponsor told Foreman. "We'll pay your daily fee and expenses, and you can take the day off." "Not a chance," responded Foreman. "We're going to call on your customers together and get as many as we can to enlist in your next training event." The sponsor learned a great lesson as Foreman's passion and never-say-die spirit turned customer resistance into "customers registered."

Making It Real

Margery Williams's *Velveteen Rabbit* is a children's book many parents have shared as a bedtime fairy tale. The dialogue between the wise Skin Horse and naive Rabbit contains great lessons for leaders. "Real isn't how you are made," said the Skin Horse to the Rabbit. "It's a thing that happens to you. . . . It doesn't happen all at once, you become. It takes a long time. That's why it doesn't often happen to people who break easily, have sharp edges, or who have to be carefully kept."

And so it is with leaders. Becoming "real" is an unfolding, accomplished in increments by taking risks, showing more of your true self, and opening up to your associates so they'll be more open in return. Before long, facades are cast aside and more meaningful connections are made. And it's only through building that kind of bond—where leaders and employees would run through walls for one another—that exemplary customer service becomes possible.

9 Partner

"Partnership is a verb disguised as a noun. It is a force released, 'un-nouned,' when dreams connect and service is gracefully given."

—CHIP BELL

An old adage states that "Authority is the last resort of the inept . . . and frustrated." Parents who have found themselves relying on "because I said so" to direct a reluctant child understand the truth of that saying. When rank or title becomes the primary means of persuading, one has long lost the battle to effectively influence. In command-and-control or hierarchical cultures, influencing involves the simple act of giving an order. Obedient followers comply with little resistance, at least until they revolt, use sick-outs, or go on strike.

In more democratic settings, leaders resort to humanistic means to persuade. Managers influence largely by *selling*—they outline the benefits of pursuing a goal. However, these efforts usually focus on getting employees to change behaviors solely for the benefit of the organization, and rarely do they emphasize why such actions may benefit workers as well. To the rank and file, such persuasion often translates to working harder simply to line executives' or shareholders' pockets.

"Colorful communication" can be another powerful tool for influencing. Communication-dependent leaders often rely on their charismatic and forceful styles to influence. But if charisma were the sole prerequisite for effective leadership, organizations would hire talented thespians to run the ship.

Role modeling is yet another common way to influence. Leaders who "walk the talk" demonstrate that whatever they are doing should be emulated. But too often that results in leaders being placed on pedestals, which does little to bolster the self-reliance of employees. The longer followers rely on a messiah-like shepherd to make all of the tough decisions or solve difficult customer problems, the further away they move from personal empowerment and accountability.

Finally, monetary and nonmonetary incentives are often used as a means to motivate and influence. Leaders often reward the "good children" among employees who act in sync with their goals and their personal vision of how business should be done. That causes rifts in the organization between employees who are favored and those who management labels as problem children.

Given some of the drawbacks of these approaches, what does a leader have left in the toolkit as a means of influencing? Finding new answers to this age-old question involves letting go of traditional notions about effective leadership.

It entails choosing *partnership* over *patriarchy*. When leaders begin to see their subordinates as partners in the act of serving customers rather than as foot soldiers to be commanded, it is then that they begin to create commitment and not just compliance.

Collective Creation of Purpose

The first step in partnering is the collective creation of purpose. In his book *Stewardship,* performance consultant Peter Block states, "The traditional process is that management creates its vision and then the enrollment process begins. . . . Enrollment is soft-core colonialism, a subtle form of control through participation. Nothing has changed in the belief in control, consistency and predictability, only the packaging is different."

It's not easy for leaders, conditioned to calling the shots and charged with "charting the course," to embrace a vision that is crafted collectively. Doing so requires involving *everyone* in the dialogue about corporate or unit direction. More importantly, it means giving that input careful consideration rather than simply going through the motions and checking off the box marked "gathered feedback."

The Power of Shared Legacy

Helping people see the critical role they play in company success—regardless of their place on the corporate food chain—is a vital role of any leader. For organizations with a long or storied history, creating a link to the past is another powerful motivational tool.

A CEO we know addressed his managers this way during a crucial juncture in the company's life. "We stand today on the shoulders of the pioneering giants who came before us," he told them. "They made this company what it is today. But you are the people on whose shoulders others will stand in the future. Let us all make sure the quality of our work ensures those who stand upon us have a sound footing."

Great leaders don't let employees forget their corporate ancestry—not in attempts to perpetuate a "We've always done it this way" approach, but rather to honor the emotional ground on which the organization stands.

Joint Accountability

Partnerships are first and foremost power-free relationships. In the best cases, they represent a marriage of equals, with each partner applying unique talents to the pursuit of a common vision—and all assuming accountability for results. Partnering by definition requires that leaders relinquish their caretaking roles and give their associates a greater say in decision-making.

In the late 1980s, Fred Smith, CEO of Federal Express, spearheaded efforts by his senior officers to capture a coveted Malcolm Baldridge National Quality Award. Knowing that the executive team would need to function as a partnership, Smith opted to focus on twelve critical measures of quality, rather than on the single "on-time deliveries" metric. Smith assigned each executive one of the measures to champion. Thus, the head of human resources, for example, might be in charge of monitoring the "Number of

Packages Pounded to Pulp" metric. If the company didn't accomplish its goals in all twelve areas, none of the executives would qualify for a bonus, which amounted to a significant percentage of their take-home pay. In the plan's first year, FedEx missed a few of the goals and every senior leader (including Smith) pocketed far less than they might have with 100 percent success. In 1990, having learned a lesson or two about partnering to foster quality, the company took home a Baldridge award. The performance leapfrogged them into industry dominance.

The Value of Honesty

In effective partnerships, honesty and candor are viewed as tools for growth—when provided in the right spirit. Partners serve each other straight talk seasoned with compassion and care. Partners take ownership of their own mistakes, work to expose—rather than cover up—service problems so they don't become chronic issues, and give each other feedback designed solely to improve performance, not criticize personality or character. If a service worker is experiencing personal or health problems that affect his performance—or is having difficulty dealing diplomatically with a "customer from hell"—he knows he can be honest with a partner leader about the situation and not risk recrimination or punitive measures.

Crafting a relationship built on honesty isn't for the weak of heart. It involves the courage to ask for unvarnished feedback and the skill to deliver it in constructive and compassionate ways. The truth may be hard to hear, but when delivered—and taken—in the right spirit, it almost always leaves partnerships stronger and more effective, as well as customers better served.

At its core, partnering is a commitment to a dialogue rather than unilateral action. It starts with asking for input rather than offering instruction, and it continues with enlisting others in problem resolution rather than positioning yourself as the sole "answer person." Partnering is operating with the faith that wisdom lies within us all and that by tapping the collective brainpower of all associates, leaders can become far more powerful and effective than by operating on their own.

10
Mentor

> "Leaders are more powerful role models when they learn than when they teach."
>
> —ROSABETH MOSS KANTER

Mentor. The word conjures up pictures of a seasoned corporate sage counseling a young employee. But what is mentoring, really? In simple terms, a mentor is someone who helps someone else learn something important. It has little to do with rank or level in an organization. Peers often mentor peers. Mentors are learning coaches and trusted advisors.

Too often, mentoring is restricted to formal programs characterized by monthly or quarterly meetings between mentor and protégé. For mentoring to have real impact, however, we believe it should be an everyday event in organizations. In the words of *The Living Company* author Arie De Geus, "Your ability to learn faster than your competition is your only sustainable competitive advantage."

Partners in Learning

When viewed through a partnering lens, mentoring is fundamentally different from the traditional, "I'm the guru, you're the greenhorn" approach. The mentors-as-partners concept means "We are fellow travelers on this journey toward wisdom." For example, one of the greatest gifts a leader can give a Loyalty Creator is to position the Loyalty Creator as his or her mentor, allowing the associate to educate the *leader* on best-in-class caretaking practices and share frontline knowledge that the manager may be removed from.

Mentoring is primarily about the transfer of knowledge, providing advice, feedback, and suggestions for improvement. But when it comes to mentoring Loyalty Creators, such wisdom isn't always received with open arms. Recall the last time someone said to you, "Let me *give* you some advice" or "I need to *give* you a little feedback." You likely did more resisting than rejoicing; few of us find unsolicited advice easy to accept. Loyalty Creators are no different.

Smart mentors create a *readiness* for the act of mentoring. Loyalty Creators are more likely to embrace offered knowledge if it's delivered in a spirit of equality, advocacy, and safety—and when the Loyalty Creator has first signaled that she is ready to receive it. Mentoring from a partnership perspective entails four stages:

1. Leveling the learning field
2. Fostering acceptance and safety
3. Giving learning gifts
4. Bolstering self-direction and independence

The first two stages are designed to grease the skids for the main mentoring event, the third stage of gifting. The final stage is about weaning the Loyalty Creator from dependence on the learning coach.

Stage 1: Leveling the Learning Field

The leader's first challenge is to help the Loyalty Creator experience the relationship as a true partnership. Leveling the learning field means stripping the relationship of any nuance of mentor power and command. It requires creating kinship and removing the mask of supremacy.

The word "rapport" means "a bringing back" or "connection renewed," and the figurative translation is "kinship." The initial mentor-caretaker encounters can make or break the quality of the relationship. Learning won't occur until the shield has been lowered enough for the learner to take risks in front of the mentor, and such shield lowering is expedited when mentors refrain from judging or lecturing in the first few interactions (as well as throughout the relationship).

It's crucial that mentors strive to use welcoming tones and nonjudgmental language in their interactions. Open posture, a warm and enthusiastic reception, direct eye contact, removal of physical barriers, and personalized greetings are all gestures that communicate a level learning field. Mentors who play the power card (peering over an imposing desk, making Loyalty Creators wait outside their office, using body language that telegraphs distance) make it difficult for any authentic or meaningful exchange to take place.

Simple statements like, "I'm here to learn as much from you as you are from me" also help to create a feeling of equality.

Stage 2: Fostering Acceptance and Safety

Great mentors show acceptance through focused and dramatic listening; they also avoid parental postures, admonitions, or tones. When it's time to listen, leaders make it their only priority, committing to mentoring engagements only when they are sure there will be no distractions. A wise leader once said, "There are no individuals at work more important to your success than your associates . . . not your boss, not your customers, not your vendors."

When a Loyalty Creator needs to bend your ear, pretend you just got a gift of five minutes with your greatest hero. Think about it. If you could have five minutes, and *only* five minutes, with Moses, Mozart, or Mother Teresa, would you let a call from your boss, your customer, or *anyone* eat up part of that precious time? Treat your associates with the same focus and priority.

Good listening is complete absorption. Watch Larry King interview guests on his CNN show. His success as an interviewer lies not so much in asking tough questions as in his terrific listening skills. He zips right past the interviewee's words, sentences, and paragraphs to get to the person's message, intent, and meaning.

The goal of a mentor should be empathetic identification. Empathy is different from sympathy. The word sympathy is derived from the Greek word meaning "shared suffering." Relationship strength is not spawned by "Misery loves company." It is built, rather, through the kind of "I have been there as well" identification that defines empathy.

Mentors do not just listen; they listen *dramatically*. That means they demonstrate through their words and actions that the words of Loyalty Creator spirits are valued and important. When people feel heard, they feel valued. Feeling valued, they are more likely to take risks and experiment, behaviors that are essential to stimulating creativity and innovation in organizations.

Stage 3: Giving Learning Gifts—Advice and Feedback

Leveling the learning field and fostering acceptance lay the groundwork for the main event: giving learning gifts. Great mentors give many gifts, including support, focus, courage, and affirmation. But none is more important than advice and feedback.

Offering advice should start with some statement of intent. It might sound like this: "George, I wanted to talk with you about the fact that your last-quarter call rate was up, but your sales were down 20 percent." But it's essential that the statement also asks permission to give advice; as mentioned earlier, nothing can grate as much as uninvited, "You need to try it my way" suggestions. This might sound like, "I have a few ideas on how we can improve this if you think they'd be helpful." The goal is to communicate in a way that doesn't make Loyalty Creators feel small or incompetent. State your advice in the first person singular. Phrases like "you *ought* to" quickly raise listener hackles. Keeping your advice in the first person singular—"what *I've* sometimes found helpful" or "what's worked for *me*"—helps eliminate the "shoulds" and removes Loyalty Creators from the defensive.

While advice giving is about *enhancing* existing skills or knowledge, feedback is more about *filling a blind spot*. As such, feedback can be more challenging to give Loyalty Creators, since it suggests a lack of skill or knowledge, which is often hard for people to acknowledge.

Admitting to your own flaws or struggles with tasks or responsibilities can make Loyalty Creators more receptive to feedback. Comments like, "I have difficulty with that myself" or "That challenged me too when I was in your position" help Loyalty Creators relate to you and open channels to receiving suggestions, rather than clogging them with defensive thoughts.

State the rationale for your performance feedback, and then assume it is *you* who is receiving the critique. In other words, deliver it in the way you would be most likely to accept it without getting overly defensive or prickly. It's important for the feedback to be straightforward and honest; sugar-coating it or telling half-truths does neither mentor nor protégé any favors. However, frankness isn't about cruelty—it's about ensuring the receiver doesn't walk away wondering, "What did he or she *not* tell me that I needed to hear?" or "That feedback was so vague I don't know where I stand or in what areas I need to improve." Be clear and specific.

Stage 4: Bolstering Self-Direction and Independence

Effective mentoring relationships are rich, engaging, and intimate. As such, it's often difficult to see them end. But like all teaching scenarios, it's healthy for the protégé to eventually leave the nest.

Make sure to celebrate the relationship before it concludes. It need not be a big, splashy event; something as simple as a special meal together or a drink after work can serve as a meaningful wrap-up. The rite of passage is a powerful symbol in gaining closure and moving on to the next learning plateau.

Leaven the celebration with laughter, stories, and joy. The Loyalty Creator now needs your blessing far more than your brilliance, your well-wishing more than your warnings. Your best contribution is a solid send-off rendered with confidence and compassion. Letting go is rarely comfortable, but it's crucial to enable the Loyalty Creator to flourish and grow out of the shadow of a mentor—to emerge as a self-directed learner who one day takes an employee of his own under his wing, keeping the powerful cycle of mentoring alive and well.

11
Align

"We need to learn to set our course by the stars, not by the lights of every passing ship."

—OMAR BRADLEY

Bridge builders are essential to the emotional and financial health of organizations—and they are ultimately key to creating customer loyalty. As individual units and their leaders acquire power and grow more insular, silos naturally begin to form in companies, triggering turf battles. Against this backdrop, bridge builders do the vital work of keeping the organization from splintering and warring against itself. Their charge is to keep the diverse factions of an organization aligned and in pursuit of shared goals.

When work requires cooperation or hand-offs across departmental lines, it's natural to favor your own unit over the goals of other groups. Communication between silos can be like speaking different languages—the message often gets lost in the translation. Since people are evaluated and compensated primarily on individual or unit performance, not inter-departmental teamwork or organizational results, other departments are often seen as the competition. But such a view can undermine service quality because ultimately it's customers who suffer when energy or resources that should be devoted to their satisfaction are consumed by internal spats and turf conflicts.

Focus on a Higher Purpose

A key to building bridges in organizations—to get departments and units "rowing together as one"—is to remind people of their collective purpose. When Ed Zander became the new CEO of Motorola Corp., the company's internal units were warring tribes fighting each other harder than they fought the competition. There was little cooperation, bad blood, and divisional strategies that worked at cross-purposes; many Motorola units even had separate booths at trade shows. Zander reunited Motorola under one flag and refocused the company on creating breakthrough products. The result of his bridge building was a far more integrated and formidable company; the payoff included a revenue increase of 25 percent and net income up over 50 percent between the time he took the helm in the first quarter of 2004 and the third quarter of 2005.

Model Great Partnering

Bridge-building leaders focus more on the greater good than on one-upping the competition or promoting partisan causes. Partnering effectively across departmental lines requires keeping promises, showing respect, seeing situations through others' eyes, and demonstrating a commitment to the relationship. It includes crafting protocols and agreements that ensure understanding and minimize dissension. It also requires valuing the whole as much as the sum of the parts, and using metrics that effectively gauge collective toil. When CEO Fred Smith focused each of his top FedEx executives on a specific area of quality with individual metrics, yet tied all of their (and his) incentive compensation to meeting the goals in all twelve areas, he created an environment in which working as partners for the collective success of the entity was the only path to success.

Focus on the Relationship

Great service leaders know that if they nurture relationships with peers, employees, suppliers, and customers, results will follow. "Successful partnerships are not built on deals and contracts," says Marriott CEO Bill Marriott, Jr. "They work because of the heart and soul of the relationship." Long-term win-win partnerships are spawned from informal covenants that guide values and behavior, not just outcomes and results. The values of honesty, reliability, passion, and support are as vital as goals, roles, rules, and accountability.

Relationship building sometimes requires extreme acts of empathy to cement the bond. "You are not eligible to change my view," states an ancient Buddhist saying, "until you demonstrate you understand my view." The walk-a-mile-in-my-shoes philosophy calls for more than a tacit appreciation of opposing perspectives—sometimes it requires bold actions. When Nelson Mandela appointed people who had once been bitter enemies to his cabinet in the South African government, it was the ultimate act of bridge building and forgiveness.

Create Settings for Interdependence

The movie *Remember the Titans*, based on a true story, is filled with alignment and bridge-building lessons. Coach Herman Boone is the newly appointed African-American coach of a Virginia high school football team in its first season as a racially integrated squad. In his first move as coach, Boone takes the team to a summer football camp and makes white players room with black players. While the community remains in racial conflict, the young men return from camp with new bonds of friendship and cooperation that eventually inspire their parents to rethink their views. Boone's team went on to win a state championship.

When CEO Ron DeFeo assumed leadership of Terex Corporation, a manufacturer of heavy construction equipment based in Westport, Connecticut, one of his first acts was to break down the walls that separated the company's many divisions and individual companies. DeFeo started the process with a companywide meeting, asking some 400 leaders to sit in three different sections representing their old company names. At one point DeFeo asked all three sections to shout their former company name at the same time; the result was pure noise. Then he asked them to shout the new company name—Terex—simultaneously. The resulting clarity proved symbolic for the three days of joint goal setting, joint customer strategy discussions, and joint updates on products that followed.

Engrave Character into Alignment

What it means to be the boss has changed dramatically in recent years. The old model of leader as stern, corporate parent has been usurped in many organizations by the image of the leader as supporter, enabler, even partner. As workers increasingly demonstrate the maturity and competence to operate well with limited supervision, leaders unable to let go of command-and-control styles have been replaced with those who view their relationships with associates as one of liberator, barrier remover, facilitator, and mentor.

The emergence of this new brand of leader has lowered the fear factor in many organizations, spurring greater creativity, more calculated risk taking, and creation of more breakthrough products. More employee inclusion has produced more employee commitment. A focus on coaching, delegation, and accountability has helped these new-breed leaders master the art of empowerment, or how and when to give their people "responsible freedom."

But all is not rosy in the leadership universe. The Greek root of the word "character" means "engraved." It represents the other end of the spectrum from situational ethics and is the antithesis of the morality for the moment that we still see practiced in too many organizations. Too many of today's leaders would rather lose sleep than lose face, and the dearth of values-based decisions has left many companies with a character deficit. What's needed is much greater alignment between principles and profit, as well as an understanding that good ethics and a robust bottom line aren't mutually exclusive concepts.

Transforming silos into alliances doesn't happen in days or months. Great bridge-building leaders are, above all, patient. They know that bridge building and alignment often come in the form of two steps forward, one back. Alliances are not achieved in one fell swoop. Thus good service leaders know they must move incrementally and with steady purpose to achieve the larger goal.

Liberate

"Empowerment is directed autonomy."

—ROBERT WATERMAN

Every time we hear someone exhorting leaders to "empower" employees, we remember Joe O'Toole, Chip's boss in his first job out of college. Joe was a crusty ex-union buster who had started out in the textile mills of South Carolina "kicking butts and taking names," as he liked to brag. Many an employee spent some sleepless nights worrying about an upcoming meeting with Mr. O'Toole.

One day Joe called a meeting to announce that the company was shifting to a participative management philosophy. The idea of Joe being participative was about as likely as Attila the Hun being compassionate. But Joe was a good company man. If the company wanted people to be more participative, he'd give it a try. Everyone was reassured, however, that the world as they knew it was not about to come crashing down when Joe ended the meeting with: "Our division *will* have participative management. And you'll participate, by God, or I'll fire your ass!"

Joe's heart was in the right place, but he missed the point. Like Joe, most leaders want to do the right thing. And, like Joe, some risk missing the point.

What is empowerment? Empowerment is the self-generated exercising of professional judgment and discretion on the customer's behalf. It is doing what needs to be done in the moment for customers rather than passing requests off to managers or blindly following policy. The importance of empowerment lies in the fact that customers expect you to meet their unique needs, not simply read to them from a rule book. And because they enjoy personalized service, it requires employees with the authority to zig and zag to fit the encounter to the customer's requirements.

Empowerment does not mean unlimited license to "just do whatever you need to do." It means *responsible freedom*. It means helping employees balance the freedom to go the extra mile for the customer with the responsibility of taking care of the organization, good service coupled with good stewardship. Bottom line, it means helping people develop an *ownership* mindset. It means instilling the belief that employees own any problems or questions customers have, no matter how vexing, from the moment they are presented until they are resolved.

Empowerment is not a gift given to employees by leaders. When leaders ask, "How do I empower my employees?" one gets a sense they are thinking of it as a present to tie a ribbon around. The job of the leader is to liberate. That means releasing power, not giving power. Think of it like this: Power is contained inside every employee. They just need the freedom to exercise it! Empowerment happens when leaders examine the work environment, service policies, processes, and their own leadership practices to identify and eliminate barriers that inhibit responsible freedom.

The following sections describe four common barriers that leaders must overcome to liberate employees.

Focus on What Matters Most

People put more passion and effort into their work when they feel part of an important mission or vision. When asked, "What are you doing?" the apathetic bricklayer states the obvious: "laying bricks." But the vision-inspired bricklayer answers, "I'm building a great cathedral."

Fred Smith, chairman of FedEx, believes evangelizing about the company's vision is a crucial part of his job: "You aren't just 'delivering stuff by 10:30 A.M.,'" Smith tells his people. "You transport the most precious cargo in the world—an organ for a vital transplant, a gift for a special ceremony, a factory part that may have halted a company's production lines." With that vision ringing in their heads, FedEx employees regularly do whatever is necessary to meet the company's service promise. There is a legend at FedEx that describes a driver who, reaching the final drop box on his route, discovered he did not have a key to open it. It was too late to return to his home base. So, he elected to take the box to the key. He backed his truck into the box, uprooted it from its concrete base, dragged it through the back door of the truck, and hauled it with him to his home base. All of the precious contents were delivered by deadline. The driver was reportedly celebrated for living the company vision.

While such above-and-beyond actions in pursuit of an inspirational service vision are commendable, it's important that maintaining core service offerings remains center stage. A liberating leader never lets employees take the service basics for granted. Hospital leaders know that as memorable as a great bedside manner might be to patients, it will be quickly forgotten if the environment is not impeccably clean and sterile. Bank executives know that beyond-the-call-of-duty service only counts if ATM transactions are accurately processed, customers move through teller lines quickly, and account statements contain no errors.

This is what we call service "air"—the fundamental, routine, non-sexy part of customer service. When Catalyst Ranch founder Eva Niewiadomski says that certain actions or inactions are "not allowed" by her staff, what she is really saying is, "Don't ever mess with service air." When nurse supervisors celebrate great patient care but also terminate employees for ignoring safety rules, they are safeguarding the underpinnings of great service. When bank managers passionately preach extraordinary service but then come down hard on repeated errors in customers' statements, they are protecting the core offering of the organization.

Support "Failing On Purpose"

Empowerment begins with error! Employees learn quickly whether they are empowered or not when they make a blunder. If the error is met with rebuke, it sends a very different message than if leaders view the misstep as an opportunity for learning and problem solving.

Without risk, there is no learning, no creativity, and no motivation. With risk, there are the occasional honest mistakes. It is easier to gently rein in an overzealous, go-the-extra-mile employee than to continually light a fire under an indifferent or uncaring one. Empowering is all about trust and the more associates feel leaders trust them, the greater their sense of freedom to do the right thing for customers. But with liberation comes responsibility. It is the leader's role to coach employees so they are equipped with the skill, knowledge, and confidence to make empowered decisions that serve both the customer's and the organization's best interests.

The concept of "support failing on purpose" has two important components. First, it means intentional error—failing *on purpose* or deliberately. Great leaders know employees sometimes have comfort zones that are several sizes too small. They need to be nudged to venture outside the safe, comfortable world of habit to serve customers with more ingenuity, assertiveness, or passion, accepting that their first few efforts might fall short of success.

The second component is about management support. The way failing efforts are perceived by leaders can make all the difference between an empowered climate and one characterized by fear. The best service leaders balance encouragement with education; they support efforts to please customers while gently instructing how other approaches may work better in the future.

The vision and values of the organization also can serve as guardrails with which to contain zealous but potentially irresponsible judgments by employees. Like the enterprising FedEx courier, when employees are passionate about the organization's purpose they can do great, yet still responsible, things in the name of customer service. Responsible freedom starts with educating employees about the kind of empowered actions that dovetail with the organization's values and service strategy.

Create Solution Spaces

Maria Montessori was a gifted French educator whose work formed the basis for Montessori schools throughout the world. At the core of her philosophy is "creativity through structure." The approach directs teachers to add structure to the "mindless" part of a child's learning environment—where the building blocks go, the child's place in the story circle, the layout of accessories when preparing to paint—which frees the child to funnel energy into higher-level thinking.

A "solution space" provides a framework for employee decision-making, offering clear guidance near the edges plus space for latitude and creativity in the middle. It is a way of saying to employees, "Within this space, make whatever decision you think is best for the customer. Outside the space, please check with someone else." Employees need guidelines, not unlimited license. The leader who says, "Just go do whatever you think is best," is likely demonstrating abdication, not empowerment.

Customers rarely seek to be treated as a number in their service experiences. While they clearly wish for consistency in the products they purchase or the service they experience, they also want to be treated uniquely. This requires front-line flexibility. When that unique or personalized treatment has the potential to be enchanting, it requires employees who feel they have a wide solution space in which to operate.

It is dangerous to assume employees will just know what they are and are not allowed to do—or even that they will believe you the very first time you tell them, "Yes, you can." Many employees have probably heard "No, you are not allowed" too many times in their past. Empowerment takes some getting used to—for both leaders and employees. It takes frequent and candid feedback. It also requires encouraging rather than denigrating actions that fail in pursuit of pleasing customers, not just celebrating results that succeed.

Drive Out Fear

What is the greatest show-stopper of service ingenuity? It's not, as you might assume, employees' fear of supervisory reprisal—it is their fear of associate rebuke. Service workers have far more work-a-day interactions with coworkers than with the boss, thus creating more opportunities for criticism or snide remarks about above-and-beyond actions they take to please customers. While leaders cannot and should not referee every employee-to-employee interaction, they need to ensure the work environment doesn't become poisoned by negativity or backbiting. There is no greater threat to employees' willingness to assert themselves or assume responsibility for pleasing customers than a hostile or unsupportive workplace.

The menacing nature of criticism can creep slowly into a culture through simple neglect and idle tolerance. It begins when leaders turn the other way when underperforming or cynical employees hurl backhanded compliments at teammates who take empowered actions for customers. Soon more employees are playing their cards close to the chest and doing only the minimum to serve customers, out of a concern of being the subject of someone's ridicule.

Great service leaders insist on kindness and respect in the ranks. While affinity cannot be legislated, consideration certainly can be. Leaders cannot force an employee to be sincerely thoughtful, but they can clearly make gossip and backbiting a career-limiting action. Strong leadership is necessary to effectively immunize a culture against negativity.

The Ragged Edge of Empowerment

Empowerment is a never-ending journey. Leaders are often impatient with how long it takes for some employees to "pick up their power." But as associates learn more about the business and begin to demonstrate their competence, leaders will feel more comfortable entrusting them with decisions.

As a result, employees will become more proficient at handling customer problems; leaders will become more able to focus on bigger picture issues; and customers will grow more loyal.

Employees will have their challenges with empowerment. Overzealous front-line employees can make decisions without the experience or competence to do so. Empowered ignorance can devolve into anarchy. Again, the transition requires patience from both leader and employee. In other cases, some employees may not grab the brass "E" ring as rapidly as leaders prefer. It can seem a lot safer to just "do what you're told," especially if the employee has been burned in the past for an initiative that did not pan out. Employees need to learn through experience—and leader encouragement—that mistakes are tools for growth, not traps for punishment.

Wise leaders recognize how service quality soars when employees are encouraged to think like owners. Workforce morale climbs, burnout is reduced, leaders feel responsibility shared, and customer retention numbers soar as customers rave about the rare organization full of employees who are engaged, inspired . . . and empowered!

13
Inspire

"Never doubt that a small group of
thoughtful and committed people
can change the world. Indeed, it's
the only thing that ever has."

—MARGARET MEAD

Picture this. You walk out of the airport to take a taxi-cab to the hotel. The taxi driver has a sullen look, seems completely disinterested in you, plays music you dislike, and talks to his buddies on his cell phone during the entire ride. When you arrive at the hotel and ask for a receipt, he acts like he's doing you a big favor and then frowns at the tip!

Now substitute the taxi driver for any one of your employees. Do you have people who seem to hate work, drag through the day like they are barely alive, show the enthusiasm of a tree stump, talk to their buddies while ignoring customers, and then get irritated when there is no raise?

Mediocrity can usurp the energy from passion and the opportunity from initiative. Leaders who tolerate mediocrity signal that their real standards are much lower than what they and their organizations say they want and/or require. Despite some conventional management thinking, it is possible for organizations to be populated *only* by winners. The proverbial bell-shaped curve of performance—that there will always be a small percentage of superstars and an equal number who do just enough to get by—is neither an organizational necessity nor statistical requirement.

The leadership antidote to passion-free mediocrity may not be to change employees, telegraph your displeasure, or even "crack the whip." Your employees may simply need to be inspired. And one of the key roles of a leader is to provide inspiration—to be a fire-starter, igniting passion and commitment.

Let's revisit the taxi driver. We have discovered that passengers can inspire drivers to give consistently great customer service. It works like this. The first step is your own animation—choosing to demonstrate the attitude you seek from the driver. For example, be upbeat and courteous. Next, as you board the taxi, sincerely express your appreciation ("Thank you for being my driver."). Tell the driver your destination and ask if he knows the location. When he says he does, deliver affirmation ("Terrific, I am dealing with a true professional."). The final part is a bit delicate. Validation is helping the driver view his role in a larger light than just driving a taxi. Keep it upbeat and optimistic ("If you hadn't gotten me to this meeting on time, I would have lost this account. Thanks for your help!"). Upon arrival, extend your hand for a handshake and then ask for a receipt. You'll be amazed at how many fires you can start.

Animation—Inspiring Through Modeling

Animation is "the process of bringing to life." The late Chuck Jones, creator of such famous cartoon characters as Bugs Bunny, Daffy Duck, Wile E. Coyote, and Road Runner, wrote, "The secret to making a character come alive is not how you draw that particular character. It happens when everything in the frame moves with the character."

Leaders who are fire-starters start by choosing to *insert* employee inspiration instead of seething about its absence. Like the cartoonist, they do this by illustrating enthusiasm. They make "everything in the frame," including their own attitude, "move with the employee." They strive to be the inspired role model they want employees to emulate. Davy Crockett was an inspirer at the siege of the Alamo in 1836. Colonel Jim Bowie wrote in a letter to Governor Henry Smith, "David Crockett has been *animating* the men to do their duty." Remember, it is impossible to light a fire with a wet match!

Appreciation—Inspiring with Gratitude

"Thank you" is a phrase we all enjoy hearing. Most people do not hear it enough. However, instead of just saying the words, take it one step further. Let the person know exactly what he or she did that warranted your gratitude. When we were eating at a restaurant, our waiter had on a nametag plus an additional tag proclaiming him to be the "employee of the month." "Congratulations," one of us said. "What did you do to warrant such an honor?" The waiter stood quietly and then said flatly, "I guess it was my turn." He had no idea what he had done to be recognized, so he knew of no special action he was being encouraged to repeat.

A few years ago, we were consulting with a successful company whose average non-supervisory professional employee was twenty-seven years old and earned about $100,000 a year! Most were highly driven, Ivy League–educated go-getters. Yet, an employee-attitude survey revealed they regarded themselves as underrewarded. At first we thought we were dealing with young, unseasoned employees who had no idea how the real world worked. But we were wrong. "We know we are very well compensated," they told us. "We just do not feel valued and recognized for what we do!" They were living examples of the famous observation by psychologist William James: "The deepest principle of human nature is the craving to be appreciated."

Affirmation—Inspiring with Confidence

"Treat a man as he is, and he will remain as he is. Treat a man as he could be, and he will become what he should be," wrote Ralph Waldo Emerson. One of the single most powerful phenomena in human behavior is the self-fulfilling prophesy (also called the Pygmalion effect). Little is really known about why it works as it does. However, your belief in your employees, demonstrated via your behavior and attitude, has a major impact on their behavior. If you believe a person is going to be a winner and you treat her that way, she generally will not disappoint you. If you believe a person is going to be a loser, and you treat him that way, he generally will not disappoint you. It suggests how important it is to communicate high expectations through words and actions. Confident inspiration starts with an obvious belief in yourself.

Validation—Inspiring with Purpose

This is the trickiest part. Leaders can change the content by expanding the context. What this means is moving from specific to general can help someone view her world in a more optimistic, hopeful light. It's a technique that parents often use to nudge a child out of a pessimistic mindset. Thus, when Susie comes home fussing that Johnny is teasing her, Susie's mother coaches her that Johnny doesn't realize how very special she really is. The intent is elevating the focus to a grander, more glorious view.

In March 2005, Wendy's became the target of a hoax that made the company the subject of the six o'clock news and wisecracks on late-night talk shows. A diner claimed she had found a fingertip in a bowl of Wendy's chili. The woman who made the claim is now facing jail time for a felony conspiracy and attempted grand theft. However, between the news of the incident and the report of the verdict, CEO Jack Schuessler wrestled a public relations bear. The way the hoax was handled by leadership elevated the pride of practically every Wendy's employee. In an interview, CEO Schuessler was asked what guidance Wendy's used to rescue their reputation. "We just stuck to our core values, doing the right thing, searching out for the truth and listening to the facts." As a leader, you can play a similar role. You have a chance to be a fire-starter—to inspire someone to deliver their very best *by living the organization's mission*.

Judy and Jane were working together in New York City and checked into a midtown hotel one evening. However, their approaches to check-in were completely different. Judy warmly approached the desk clerk with a Steinway smile and a jovial disposition. She made complimentary small talk with the clerk, using the name she had eyeballed on his uniform jacket. Jane took a more somber route with a desk clerk at the other end of the counter. She made little eye contact or small talk, put her credit card on the counter, filled out the paperwork in silence, and departed with a room key.

The plan was for the two women to go to their respective rooms, drop their luggage, and then rendezvous in Judy's room to go out for dinner. But when Jane entered Judy's room, she was stunned. Judy had a suite four times the size of Jane's standard hotel room, plus it had a great view of Central Park.

"How did you get this big suite?" Jane inquired of her colleague. Judy humbly responded, "I wanted more than a typical room. I knew the front desk clerk really wanted me to have it; I just needed to inspire him." The story doesn't end there. When the two women returned from dinner, Judy's message light was on. It was the front desk clerk who had called to make sure her suite was satisfactory. Needless to say, Jane's message light wasn't blinking.

Inside every employee is passion waiting to be ignited, excellence ready to be released. Strike your leadership match—animation, appreciation, affirmation, and validation—and be warmed by the results.

14
Champion

Service leaders who serve as champions know their
role is about making employees' hearts happy, not a
precise set of reward or recognition "to do's." Champions are the likes of Clint Eastwood in the movie
Million Dollar Baby, Tom Cruise in *Jerry McGuire*, and
Denzel Washington in *Remember the Titans*—all characters who supported and sought the best in others,
even in their darkest hours. Championing isn't necessarily about applause, cheers, or approval. All of
those actions may be present, but championing makes
someone feel *treasured*, not just appreciated.

We began writing this book thinking that the seventh key Loyalty Creator leadership skill was "Celebrate," and were convinced that applause was the
ticket to igniting Loyalty Creator wannabes to deliver
superb service. But as we talked with managers who

championed the likes of Loyalty Creators Daryl, Richard, Sherri, and Dave, we realized they were doing far more than giving public pats on the back. They displayed a sincere allegiance to the targets of their affection. They also showed a readiness to sponsor, support, and defend. Thus "celebrate" morphed into "champion."

Great leaders focus on the effect they are trying to create, not on the set of recognition tasks they are supposed to "check off." It's much like empowerment. Leaders don't embed power; they remove the barriers to power. They don't motivate, they create conditions that help employees motivate themselves. In much the same way, great leaders don't merely recognize or appreciate; they nourish spirit by whatever means necessary. That is the role of the champion. The by-product of championing is enhanced employee self-esteem, confidence, pride, and commitment. Champions focus more on the outcome of their efforts and less on the process used. Two examples will help illustrate the difference.

The CEO of a large manufacturing company was expected to make an appearance at an annual employee recognition dinner. His chief of staff had carefully prepared his remarks, including researching a bit of personal information about each award winner. The goal was to make the audience believe that the CEO knew every winner personally. But the carefully choreographed charade came unraveled when one of the honored employees had the same name as an employee who had been forcefully retired a few weeks earlier. The awkward moment came when the CEO departed from his script and commented that he was surprised to see the person on the stage since he had thought he was on his way to the golf course in his retirement. That's an example of contrived, process-focused championing going awry.

Now let's consider the opposite case. We were at a retirement banquet a few years ago as guests of a client. Every aspect of the ceremony was well-trodden ground—until the final retiree was announced. For this person the applause was longer, the smiles broader, and the spirits higher.

The object of the crowd's affection was a security officer retiring after forty years with the organization. The company president asked the man to come up onto the massive stage, and the audience hushed as the security officer's many accomplishments were listed. The president then announced a special gift for this special retiree. The suspense was palpable. What kind of present could appropriately celebrate the contributions this man had made to so many?

The first clue was the buzz from the back of the room as a man appeared in the doorway. We could hardly believe our eyes! Down the long aisle from the back door to the podium walked one of the most famous people in the business world. His face was familiar to everyone in the room—and, for that matter, probably everyone in the country.

The surprise visitor walked straight to the security officer and embraced him warmly. With tears falling from his eyes, he thanked the retiree for being a wonderful tutor during his two-year stint with the organization much earlier in his career. After a few short stories about their association, he left the banquet hall to board his limo and jet back to the opposite coast. The crowd sat stunned—no one spoke for a long time. Then, one by one, they filed to the front to express their gratitude to all of the retirees.

Advocate, Don't Just Celebrate

Did you ever have someone who believed in you unconditionally even though you didn't feel you deserved such backing? A celebrator recognizes and affirms what you *accomplish*, but a champion shows respect and admiration for *who you are* and believes in you when others may have written you off. A champion campaigns on your behalf, backs you against all odds, and defends you against all foes. The concept of leader as champion goes far beyond the usual affirmation. Champions do not view their role as cheerleader; they see themselves more as stewards of reputation.

Align Advocacy with Vision

When famed tennis coach Mike Estep talks about his role as the coach of tennis great Martina Navratilova, he focuses on bringing out the very best in his client. He also speaks of elevating her playing to match the greatness of the game itself. Tiger Woods credits his late father, Earl, with helping him think about making an impact on the world beyond golf and his awe-inspiring athletic feats. Mike Estep and Earl Woods, great champions both, zeroed in on a vision of greatness that was much more than the sum of the competitor and the contest. Champions are committed to a service vision and use it as a tool not only to direct and align performance, but to affirm and motivate employees as well.

Champions Don't "Affirm Conditionally"

One of Chip's first jobs out of college was as a management trainee in a bank. He started his rotational training program working as a teller. After he had mastered that job, the branch manager assigned him to train a new teller—a woman twenty years Chip's senior who had just come from another bank. She was also someone who appeared to have used up her supply of smiles in the job interview.

Armed with a new college degree and a grand total of thirty-four days of work experience, Chip thought he was hot stuff. But his freshman attempts at affirmation came to a screeching halt when he placed a loud "but . . ." at the end of a compliment he delivered about the woman's work. She slowly rose to her feet and coldly looked Chip over from head to toe. "Young man, you can never boss me! I was bossing when you were just a gleam in your father's eye." With that declaration, she marched into the branch manager's office and demanded a transfer. Chip never dreamed that one single word—"but"—could render an attempt to affirm so ineffective and inflammatory.

Conditional affirmation ("Patsy, you're doing a great job, *but* . . .") turns the receiver deaf to the positive piece of the commentary. And if the critique carries parental tones, power and status issues are also raised. So what do the best leaders do? They separate praise and criticism. If your goal is to praise, then praise. If your goal is to critique, then critique. Mixing the two in the same sentence or session can turn a confirming pat on the back into a controlling kick in the pants.

PART THREE

SUSTAINING REMARKABLE SERVICE

Changing the beliefs, habits, and practices of people takes patience, sensitivity, and tenacity. It also requires a methodology that is steeped in the tenets of organizational psychology and human systems change management. Employees rarely change because of organizational mandates. Change happens instead when individuals are motivated from within to approach their work differently—when they clearly see what's in it for them, as well as the organization, to adopt new mindsets or behaviors.

Creating customer-centric cultures starts with an intimate understanding of customers—their needs and expectations as well as hopes and aspirations—and continues with crafting a clear service vision. A vision is not simply a collection of lofty phrases and high-minded words on a poster or back of a business card. It is a shared picture of business success and competitive advantage that guides the actions of all employees from the senior executive to the security guard. A clear vision helps leaders and employees make choices among many initiatives competing for their time and attention. It also is the foundation for standards, norms, metrics, and structures that govern external and internal customer service.

Culture change isn't for the impatient or easily derailed; developing a service-focused organization requires constant care and feeding from leaders and a resilient spirit that views setbacks as natural stepping stones to success.

Crafting a remarkable service culture requires a number of stages, some of which can unfold simultaneously with others. Following is our proven process for creating such a culture.

Crafting a Remarkable Service Culture

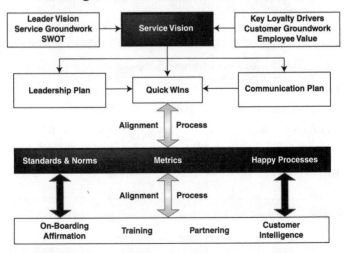

A *service vision* describes the totality of the customer experience—how it looks, sounds, feels, or tastes from the customer's eyes. It reflects four inputs:

- Key loyalty drivers, or those parts of the customers' experiences that have the biggest impact on their decisions to keep doing business with the company
- Employee value, or the capacity of the vision to resonate with and motivate employees
- SWOT, or the strengths, weaknesses, opportunities, and threats unique to the organization
- Leader vision, or a strategy for success that reflects the best thinking and passion of those at the top of the organization

Two additional inputs are key to crafting the service vision. Service groundwork is an activity where leaders spend time on the front lines to learn first-hand about customer experiences; customer groundwork refers to leaders standing in the shoes of customers to view the organization through their eyes.

Enacting the Vision

A service vision leads to creation of a detailed leadership plan—the articulation of select practices and initiatives to be guided through the management chain of command. The vision also lays the groundwork for the communication plan—how the service strategy and the value of service excellence are communicated throughout the organization. One key to culture change is what we call *extraordinary* communication—communication from leadership that goes beyond the norm to help keep service priorities "top of mind" for employees. *Quick wins* (from the leadership plan as well as the communication plan) are timed to signal to all, in literal and symbolic ways, that change is achievable, real, and important.

The sequence of these stages is crucial. All are a part of an alignment process that helps "everything in the frame to move with the main character." Service standards, norms, and metrics need to be in sync with the service vision. The vision also guides the alignment and integration of key business processes. It shapes and informs on-boarding (selection, placement, and orientation of new employees), training, customer intelligence (real-time and periodic customer feedback), and more. Developing partnership protocols is crucial to ensuring aligned results and cooperation (not siloed activity) among different business units. Finally, all manner of affirmation processes (employee recognition, incentives, balanced scorecards, compensation, and so on) need to be aligned with and flow from the vision, standards, norms, and metrics.

To be truly effective, the entire process also must be realigned and updated as customer requirements change and the new customer-centric organization matures. Taken together, all of these elements add up to an exceptional service culture that provides a natural barrier to the competition and keeps customers coming back in droves.

15 Harness Intelligence

"Some see the glass as half-empty;
some see the glass as half-full. I see
the glass as too big."

—GEORGE CARLIN

Ever had a maitre d', waiter, or waitress saunter up to your table and ask the perfunctory, "How was everything?" and even though you were underwhelmed with the meal or service, you said "Fine"? If so, you have participated in one of the most meaningless efforts in modern business—the solicitation of useless customer feedback.

Evaluative customer feedback of this sort is sold to organizations as a critical tool in understanding customers' needs and expectations. This leads to a lot of money being spent on plain-vanilla customer surveys, irritating phone callers seeking interviews during dinnertime, and long-winded market research reports replete with cross tabulations and PowerPoint presentations. What's wrong with soliciting evaluative customer feedback?

It is little more than superstitious corporate behavior built on five myths:

MYTH: *A satisfied customer is a loyal customer.*
FACT: More than 75 percent of customers across all industries who leave an organization for a competitor, rated themselves as "satisfied" or "completely satisfied" with the previous organization on customer surveys. It takes more than mere satisfaction to ensure long-term loyalty.

MYTH: *If customers say they are satisfied, it's true.*
FACT: Most customers would rather tell a little lie about being satisfied than to engage in a potentially confrontational dialogue explaining why they were not happy with a product or service. Candor is not easy for people, which is why many choose flight over fight.

MYTH: *Customers want the organizations they do business with to ask them for feedback.*
FACT: Customers want organizations to read their minds! Only the raving fan or the super angry have the motivation to provide feedback. Most everyone else in between wants to be left alone.

MYTH: *Customers believe that if they give feedback, something will actually change.*
FACT: Most customers are twice-bitten cynics. Most customers believe organizations solicit feedback because they are either directed to by some edict or incented to by some prize,

not because the organization is sincerely anxious to improve. Even if improvements are made using feedback, most customers never learn of the changes, so the perceptive effect is "They don't care."

MYTH: *Complaining customers are your most at-risk buyers— the ones most likely to defect.*
FACT: Not so. It's the quietly disappointed ones you have to look out for. Those are the ones who, approached by a competitor with a shinier widget or a slightly better deal, will abandon you for bluer skies, greener pastures, and the promise of a more hassle-free experience.

Customers often view requests for their feedback as a redundant activity. They believe they are giving the organization feedback each time they buy another product or service, a different product or service, recommend you to others, or remain a customer over time. So the question remains: How can an organization stay current on customers' ever-changing needs and expectations without annoying or estranging them with traditional customer feedback efforts?

Focus on Learning, Not Evaluation

Customer feedback is about evaluation; customer learning is about *problem solving*. Problem solving means learning for improvement. Problem solving requires more customer *intelligence* than customer *evaluation*, more ideas than critique. And customers enjoy solving problems with you when they are invited. Shifting from a customer evaluation to a customer-learning focus requires new tools, new methods, and above all, new mindsets.

Rule #1: Stop expecting surveys to be tools for learning

Written customer surveys yield mildly interesting demographic and psychographic information that can, generally, be useful in marketplace positioning or strategy. But customer intelligence, the kind relevant for service or product improvement, is best achieved face-to-face and ear-to-ear.

Rule #2: Train customer contact people to ask open-ended questions

Learning begins with a spirit of openness. If customers feel free to move the conversation as they see fit, they will gravitate to areas of significance to *them*—the good, bad, and ugly of their personal experience. "What are ways we can . . . ?" or "How would you suggest we . . . ?" are much more likely to give you a lesson your customer is willing to deliver.

Rule #3: Train customer contact people to present problem-solving, non-evaluative questions

Questions that are evaluative in nature create a tone of critique—right and wrong, good and bad. Problem-solving questions can be fun for customers to answer and are generally taken seriously. Ask a customer questions like, "If this were your restaurant, what would you do differently?" And if the customer says, "I don't know," respond with a warm, "If you did know, what would you suggest!" This tells customers you are serious about their ideas.

Rule #4: Honor customers for taking the time to teach you

Most customers have no particular interest in instructing you in their perspective on your service. It is incumbent on the student (that's you) to give the customer some incentive to provide you a quick lesson. If possible, let customers know how you plan to report on the improvements made from their lessons. And if you make that promise, always keep it.

Rule #5: Listening to customers is good; watching customer behavior is even better

People often behave in ways different than they predict. When Professor Gerald Young at the University of Florida compared the reasons patients gave for switching physicians with the reasons they predicted would influence that decision, there was a major difference. "Quality of medical practice" was the factor patients consistently said would send them away, while in fact, "bedside manner" was the most frequent trigger for the change.

Customer behavior is often more telling than the customer's words. Continuum, a Massachusetts-based consulting firm, found that out when hired to conduct market research for Moen, Inc., for use in the development of a new line of showerheads. Continuum felt the best way to discover what customers wanted in a new showerhead wasn't to ask them via surveys but rather to *watch* them in action. According to the *New York Times*, the company got permission to film customers taking showers in their own homes and used the findings in the new design. Among the insights gleaned were that people spent half their time in the shower with their eyes closed and 30 percent of their time avoiding water altogether. The data contributed to the new Moen Revolution showerhead becoming a best seller.

Rule #6: Service wisdom comes from customer intelligence, not just customer feedback

Service wisdom comes from valuing an assortment of sources for customer intelligence. The security guard's assessment of the demeanor of a departing key customer can be more instructive than forty focus groups and sixty surveys; talking with a customer you lost last year might be more helpful than talking with the one you acquired last week. And never make assumptions about what the customers think. There will always be a few customers who "see the glass not as half empty or half full, but as too big!"

Rule #7: Spread your customer learning as widely as possible

Stew Leonard's Dairy in Norwalk, Connecticut, posts customer suggestions on a giant bulletin board for all to see. Managers also make copies and distribute them to key departments throughout the supermarket. USAA Insurance in San Antonio, Texas, posts customer ideas on a special section of its corporate intranet. The key is to let as many people as possible—as quickly as possible—know what customers think.

We typically think of customer feedback as judgmental opinions, not as instructive information. Consider the word itself. "Feeding back" implies nurturance, like returning important nutrients to the soil through fertilizer. Customers will more likely give you lessons that "fertilize" your customer service if you approach them as if you're a student eager for a lesson rather than as a pupil uneasy about getting a grade.

Customer Groundwork for Leaders

Leaders need to be an integral part of gathering customer intelligence. We call this practice "doing your groundwork"—it means homework with the assignment of seeing service through customers' eyes. It's one thing to read static customer satisfaction reports. It's quite another to spend time in the field gathering first-hand research. The latter—customer groundwork—can have a far greater impact on leaders' perception of service quality. Here are a few ways leaders can gather customer intelligence.

Test service processes for fissures and faults

When John Longstreet was the general manager of the Harvey Hotel in Plano, Texas, he occasionally invited frequent guests to come to his office after check-in for "secret" assignments.

These were a few of John's missions:

- "Call housekeeping at 3 A.M. and request twenty towels."
- "Ask room service for something not on the menu."
- "Break a glass in the restaurant, and let me know what happened."

The guest-investigator always received a room rate discount for his research, and John got invaluable information on how his service processes really worked.

Assume the many moods of the customer

Roberto R. Herencia, president of Chicago-based Banco Popular North America, invited his key leaders to join him for a day of shopping the bank's competition. Each senior leader was given a collection of bank branches to visit—including some Banco Popular branches. Not only were these "mystery shoppers" directed to make specific requests, they were encouraged to assume the personality of various customers—irate, uninformed, demanding, arrogant, and so on. The field research proved to be a powerful source of insight for leaders about ways to boost service quality.

Don't forget to be helpless

As challenging as high-decibel customers can be to the front line, few customer types are more unnerving (and more instructive) than the helpless customer. Explaining something a third time can cause a server to stop and reflect ("Why *do* we do it that way?"). Helpless customers make you think processes and practices through in an elemental way, which often leads to small but important improvements in service quality.

Do your homework on loyalty drivers

Pick four senior leaders and ask them which components of the organization's service experience are the biggest drivers of customer loyalty. If you get as much as a 20 percent difference in their answers, there is a need for a refresher course. Now, assume a unit or organization focused its time on improving just one of those loyalty drivers. If you looked at how service was delivered through the lens of that one feature, what would you see (or not see) that might need addressing?

In short, if you really want to provide exceptional customer service you need to really know your customers. First-hand research, not surveys, is the most reliable means of knowing what really matters to your customer base.

16
Create Consistency

> "The very essence of leadership is that you have to have vision. You can't blow an uncertain trumpet."
>
> —THEODORE HESBURGH

From the steps of the Lincoln Memorial on a hot August afternoon in 1963, Dr. Martin Luther King, Jr. delivered a well-chronicled speech. His oratory did *not* start with the words, "I have a strategic plan." The momentous word Dr. King chose instead was *dream*.

King's powerful speech was a watershed in the history of the Civil Rights movement in America. The speech gave thousands of activists a clear vision, and the words became a call to action that unified people around a shared, persuasive purpose.

While changing entrenched racial views clearly is not the same as changing organizational cultures, the preconditions to success are similar. Culture change involves helping people abandon comfortable, habitual, and often corrosive attitudes and actions for those that are new, untested, and even frightening. Such a transformation requires a vision sufficiently compelling to invite courageous action. It also demands behavioral standards and norms that promote consistency of action.

Why Start with a Service Vision?

When it comes to service, customers require consistency for trust. Texas A&M researcher Leonard Berry found that the number-one attribute customers value in the service they receive is *reliability*—an organization's ability to provide what was promised, dependably and accurately. Customers want the service from branch A to be as good as branch B; they don't like having to choose a specific location—or a specific teller, floor salesperson, or waiter—because opting for others represents a roll of the dice. They want every service encounter to live up to their expectations every time.

How do you get everyone in the organization "rowing together" as one to deliver a consistently high level of service—the kind of reliable and trustworthy performance that keeps customers coming back again and again? It starts with a compelling and actionable service vision.

Consistent service excellence demands some decision guidelines, or "anchors," that make it easy for every employee to make decisions that align with the company's overarching service mission. Creating a service vision, standards, and norms provides those critical alignment anchors.

Virtually every business book, keynote speech, or consulting proposal on culture change starts off with the admonition to "Get a vision." Yet if you ask front-line employees about the "new" vision (and its accompanying fanfare), most will reveal that such vision statements end up being framed fixtures in the company lobby, not something that directs their daily work. Thus, if everyone agrees that a clear vision is necessary to implement culture change, yet most vision efforts fail to pass the "snicker test" with rank-and-file workers, where does it falter? Is the disconnect a result of poor preparation, inadequate communication, or a flawed vision development process? The *process* of vision creation is often the most frequent culprit. Service vision success stories share four components:

- Effective service visions reflect a blend of four inputs:
  - Customer loyalty drivers; that is, those performance areas that have biggest influence on customers' repurchase intentions
  - A clear-eyed review of the unit or organization's strengths, weaknesses, opportunities, and threats
  - Leadership's own vision of what constitutes distinctive service
  - The active participation of every employee
- Leaders willing to say, "Here is our service vision, the signature experience we strive to create for our customers, and nothing is more important than 'living that vision'—nothing."
- Leaders who use the service vision as the lens through which to look at all plans, practices, and performances to ensure they are consistent with what is expected by customers. Those leaders also must be bold enough to take action when policies or processes are out of sync with the vision.

- Leaders who model service vision-aligned behaviors (and insist that others do as well) and champion modified performance management processes to evaluate and emphasize those service behaviors.

A Service Vision in Action

A clear vision is the mechanism that enables employee energies to be aligned toward exemplary service. It is the tool that helps leaders make choices among initiatives competing for their time and budgetary resources. It also provides the underpinning for all service standards, norms, metrics, and structures.

Service visions are best understood by way of example. In Chapter 4 we introduced you to Freeman, a Dallas-based company that provides services for expositions, exhibits, and corporate events. (Earlier you met Freeman employee Keith Kennedy, the Problem Solver Loyalty Creator.) Long renowned for delivering superior service to meeting planners, show managers, and association leadership, Freeman discovered that it had shortchanged a key constituency while showering attention on others—the exhibitor.

Market research indicated that treating the exhibitor as a key customer was essential to Freeman's future growth. More and more exhibitors—especially large corporate clients who exhibit at many conferences and shows a year—had a growing influence on who show management selected to manage their exhibit space. And Freeman wanted to be exhibitors' "service provider of choice."

So the company crafted a service vision to communicate a new focus and to ensure a high level of service quality for exhibitors. Freeman used four key steps to formulate the vision:

1. **Identify your key customers.** For Freeman it was, obviously, the exhibitor, not just show management.

2. **Identify the primary loyalty drivers for this key customer group.** We all know the core contribution to customers is important. For airlines, it's moving people from point A to point B, on time, safely, with luggage intact. But as we stressed in the opening of the book, delivering on those basics might yield customer satisfaction, but it doesn't necessarily create loyalty. Through its customer research Freeman learned the things that kept exhibitors loyal to the organization were unfailing accuracy, responsiveness to requests or problems, and professionalism.

3. **Decide what you want to be famous for.** A service vision ought to have some jump-start component that makes you distinctive and exciting in the eyes of customers. L.L. Bean is well known for its return policy, Amazon.com for how it personalizes the online shopping experience, and Walt Disney World for creating magical moments. Find that "secret sauce" that reflects the vision of leaders, sets you apart from competitors, and bolsters pride among employees. Freeman decided to customize more of the services it delivers to exhibitors as a way to create distinction from competitors.

4. Get lots of employees involved. Everyone from the front lines to executive suite should be asked to provide input, react to drafts, and offer suggestions about what will play with your customer base. If employees cannot find their fingerprints on the final draft of the vision, they are not likely to own it and implement it.

The service vision of Freeman ended up sounding like this: *"The service vision of Freeman is to support exhibitors, show managers, and event professionals in the successful marketing of their products and services by providing highly personalized, proactive solutions delivered through a valued relationship with trusted, accessible experts."*

Standards Bring the Vision to Life

A service vision can set the tone and inspire the troops, but it is only a starting point. People need direction, mileposts, and incremental goals to ensure their performance aligns with the vision and is consistent across the organization. Service standards grow out of the service vision. They illustrate how "The Freeman Way" or "The Acme Style" looks in thought and action in the call center, sales floor, or the checkout line.

Behaviors that consistently breed customer loyalty won't occur without company-wide standards and norms that are aligned with the service vision. Service breakdowns often happen, for example, at the intersection of two internal units that only care about their side of the equation. If there are precise, worked-out-in-advance standards about interdepartmental operations and cooperation—and if units are held accountable for meeting them—it provides a blueprint for efficient and effective execution. The overall goal is consistent practice and aligned efforts. Such consistency—delivering on promises, again and again—builds trust in customers and helps cement their loyalty to the organization.

Where Do Standards Come From?

An organization-wide standard communicates what all associates should strive to *be*, every time—so customers get a consistent style, attitude, manner, and service experience. Standards are crafted around performance dimensions that have the biggest influence on customer loyalty, as well as those factors deemed most important by the service vision.

Addressing three questions can help develop a more effective and compelling service standard:

1. What do customers value? Begin by reviewing the primary customer loyalty drivers to ensure standards are built around performance factors that customers really value, not those that have little impact on whether they decide to keep doing business with you. When research told Freeman that responsiveness to requests, questions, and problems was key to winning the loyalty of exhibitor customers, leaders transformed that finding into one of their ten service standards: *"We exist to serve and provide value to our customers by understanding their needs and delivering appropriate quality solutions on-time, first time, every time."*

2. What in the organization's culture is in need of repair? Factors associated with organizational culture can often create barriers to good service. Freeman, for example, discovered that employees too often avoided responsibility when things went wrong for customers, failing to "own" problems and see them through to effective resolution—regardless of who was to blame. A new service standard emerged to address this barrier: *"We meet our commitments to our customers and colleagues—there are no excuses. We own up to mistakes and respond proactively to find a solution."*

3. What is the organization's "special opportunity"? Service standards bring to life the "secret sauce" that makes a unit or organization stand out from its competitors. Start by asking where in the organization opportunities exist for differentiation in serving customers or colleagues. Freeman believed personalizing more of its services, and designing its service functions through the eyes of the customer, would provide a competitive edge. The standard that resulted was this: *"At Freeman we do everything with a customer-centered focus rather than for internal convenience."*

Turning Standards into Norms

While service standards are effective at establishing general guidelines and mindsets, they can be open to interpretation. Use of "norms" brings another layer of precision to the service vision by helping employees see what a standard looks like in action. Norms outline examples of behaviors and practices that demonstrate how the standard looks when applied in day-to-day service situations.

A norm describes what all associates strive to *do*, every time, in the same fashion, across the organization, so customers get consistent action, effort, or execution. Think of norms like this. If you shot a video of a colleague serving customers in a way consistent with a given standard, the resulting footage would be a norm. Ask yourself the following about the norms you have established in your organization:

- Does it prescribe an action, behavior, or practice consistent with the standard?
- Is it clear enough that all who read it will have the same understanding of how it should be applied?
- Is it stated in a way that it could be easily measured or verified?
- Is the norm applicable to service interactions with customers *and* colleagues?
- Does the norm reflect the service vision?

Freeman, for example, developed a new standard around customer feedback and how that feedback was to be used throughout the organization. Leaders then identified a collection of norms to help illustrate what that standard would look like in practice:

Standard: *We continually seek timely customer feedback. We implement changes that enhance our customers' experience and improve the ease of doing business with Freeman.*

Norms:

- We listen openly before responding to our customer.
- The voice of the customer drives our business.
- We will continually look for innovative methods of improving our customers' experience.

They also used a standard and set of norms to address the long-held tendency to focus on what worked for Freeman at the expense of what worked for customers.

Standard: *We do everything with a customer-centered focus rather than for internal convenience.*

Norms:

- We stop and take care of the customer even if the customer interrupts us in the middle of a task.
- We always look for ways to make the customers' experience easier.
- We ensure our internal focus is customer driven.

Completing the Blueprint for Customer Loyalty

Just as an organization might have a price, product, or competitive strategy, it is vital that they also have a service strategy. After drafting a service vision, standards, and norms, it can be helpful to assemble a cross-functional team to create an *initial* service strategy implementation plan (SSIP). A typical initial SSIP includes a leadership plan, as well as a communications and rollout plan for cascading the service vision, standards, and norms throughout the organization, as well as the initiation of an ongoing alignment process.

There's no shortage of research into what makes for great service leadership; the studies, books, and articles could likely fill a vast warehouse. We have seen executives fund and preside over service visioning retreats that produce extraordinary prose yet eventually end up in the "project of the month" file. We believe three ingredients—dream, drive, and daring—are required for the service greatness recipe.

Ideating a Service Vision

Creating a unique service vision is a special challenge, and the difficulty often grows if leaders go into a vision-development effort with a strategic planning mentality. Where planning requires a logical approach, creating a vision demands a more inventive and boundless tact. Following are some questions and exercises that can help get leaders in the right frame of mind for developing a distinctive service vision:

A. What would you do to create a unique service experience for your customers:
- If you had unlimited resources?
- If you were a superhero with supernatural powers?
- If you wanted to invent an experience completely different from any other on the planet?
- If you were going to name your business unit in honor of your parents, son, or daughter?

B. Describe what the new service experience sounds like, looks like, smells like, feels like, or tastes like.

What memorable sensory experience do you want to create for customers?

C. Select a folk hero or other prominent person that might be most representative of the new service experience you want to create. If that character were to provide advice on crafting the new experience, what would he or she recommend?

D. When you think of the service experience:
- What one positive emotion or feeling do you want customers to walk away with?
- What organization currently does a world-class job of making its customers feel the emotion you selected?
- How do you think that company would design your service experience to ensure your customers feel the same way as theirs do?

17
Start Quick Wins

Watching a skilled magician at work is an exercise in awe. Try as we might to figure out the trick behind the sleight-of-hand illusions, we still come away amazed and astonished. Where did those cards fly off to? Where did that dove come from? We know in our minds there is a rational explanation. But in our hearts we aren't so sure.

Cultural transformation is in part organized magic. Just as the stage magician turns a playing card into a flower or live pigeon, the process of transforming an inwardly focused unit or enterprise into a customer-centered one can seem just as mysterious. However, if you videotaped a magician at work (or a culture in change) and reviewed the tape in slow motion, what appears to be magic would instead show itself to be a disciplined attention to focus and timing.

Deliberate culture change typically begins far from the factory floor or bullpen of cubicles. Instead, culture change is often instigated in the executive suite by managers who unilaterally decide that the corporate culture should be different.

Grass-roots change does occasionally happen. But because it can be viewed by those in charge as upsetting the stability of the organization, grass-roots change is generally seen as borderline mutiny to be stopped before it gathers momentum. In his groundbreaking book *Stewardship,* author Peter Block compares employee-led (as opposed to leader-led) culture change to a foreign object that enters some part of the body. The body senses invasion and sends out armies of white blood cells to extract or neutralize the intruder. Bottoms-up change efforts often encounter similar resistance as the organization seeks to contain and quell it.

Culture change is sometimes (and should always be) inclusive, but it is rarely led by front-line employees. Thus, it seldom features the quantity of employee participation that can turn doubt into belief. Absent their authorship or extensive participation, employees see the transformational magic as a trick—a con concocted by some corporate Merlin for some unpleasant purpose. "This is really about doing more with less, isn't it?" they commiserate with their colleagues. Or, they hunker down with quiet, indifferent compliance and an all-knowing resolution that "This too will soon pass."

Skepticism is a huge challenge to implementing cultural change. Add to that the in-slow-motion nature of change and you have a recipe for downright defiance. Thus, you need a planned bridge to make the magic work. The magician's label for such a bridge is "carefully timed misdirection." Misdirection is a fundamental tactic of magic: The magician who gestures and looks off to the left of the audience is almost always moving the audience's attention to where the trick is not happening—or to be precise, away from where the effect is subtly being set up or staged.

Misdirection is a frequent phenomenon in everyday life as well, although we usually don't notice it. The nurse asks about the patient's weekend while giving a flu shot; the bellman calls the guest's attention to a beautiful plant opposite the site of new hotel construction; the dentist chitchats about his latest ski trip while applying a shot of Novocain—all are instances of misdirection.

The Quick Win: Timed Misdirection

Quick wins in the corporate world are a signal to all, in literal and symbolic ways, that the change is real, achievable, and legitimate. Quick wins are short-term improvement projects clearly related to the culture change initiative that demonstrate success for the change initiative as well as provide authentic differences in service performance from past approaches.

Quick wins are service vision–aligned initiatives that provide high impact and high visibility results of enhanced service to external customers or internal colleagues. Some examples include the following:

- A financial services firm revising levels of check approval and lending authority to provide clients in their branches with more efficient service.
- A large firm learns from employee focus groups that its employee directory is either out of date or missing thus making it difficult for employees to assist customers, particularly when customer requests require cross functional involvement. The company implements a "crash program" to get the information updated and available on an intranet site as quickly as possible.
- An organization realized it created unacceptably long wait times in its customer service centers by failing to communicate alternative methods for requesting service orders to their customers. Leaders rapidly implemented an improved communications program for customers that provided alternative methods of requesting service—and dramatically lowered customer wait times.

Quick wins are not deceptive acts, but they are diversionary. The nurse's success in diverting the patient's attention away from the flu shoot only works if the query about the patient's weekend is perceived as authentic. We allow the magician to divert our gaze to a peripheral or nonessential part of a trick only because we are convinced such guidance is legitimate. And it is. We are rewarded for our gullibility—not by feeling manipulated, but by becoming enchanted.

In much the same way, quick wins divert employees away from the seemingly never-ending nature of culture change. When workers respond with comments like, "Things really are happening," you know the quick-win concept is working. Quick wins give immediately visible results and divert employees away from the belief that the culture change is purely cosmetic.

Are "quick wins" the change effort itself? No, they are a small part of the effort. However, because of their timing and because of their particular focus, they have a clout much greater than similar interventions that aren't carried out under the banner of culture change. They also are crucial to laying the foundation for more lasting change. Here are quick-win principles for ensuring success.

Choose a Crowd-Pleasing Quick Win

Quick wins work if they are easily identified with the service excellence culture change effort and are closely aligned with delivering the unique service experience described in your service vision. They work if the projects or initiatives selected are highly visible and easily understood by employees. Quick wins are worthwhile if they have an unquestioned impact or benefit on how customers experience the service or how employees experience internal support.

Timing Can Make or Break Quick Wins

Make sure quick wins are timed to get the biggest bang for the buck. They should be executed early in the culture change effort to demonstrate early leadership commitment and to begin delivering on promises of improved service experiences to customers and employees. Implement them at a time when skepticism may be running high and resources are available. If people are preoccupied with other organization-wide programs, such as a core system or technology change, the quick win may get lost or overshadowed by competing priorities. Effective timing and impact can be assured by involving employees, customers, and suppliers in selecting the best quick-win projects.

Use a Natural Event to Energize Quick-Win Implementation

Associate the quick win with a happy moment. Announce the implementation of the quick win as a part of celebrating the successful completion of an improvement initiative; after announcing the acquisition of a major new customer; while celebrating individual performance such as the announcement of promotions, employees of the month/quarter/year, and long-term employee anniversaries; or as a part of "where do we go from here" discussions of outstanding organizational results in revenue and profitability. Here's one note of caution: Be sure to separate quick-win initiatives from any results that included substantial workforce reductions. Employees will inevitably link the quick-win project with the prospect of further downsizing.

Watch Out for Leader Whiplash

If designed poorly, quick wins can require more time or energy from leaders than they initially expect. Additionally, quick wins can meet leader resistance if they upset a vital power setup or the status quo. The most successful quick wins are those obvious small changes that, when completed, dramatically improve the service experience of your customer. Be vigilant for leaders mistakenly thinking the quick win is the real culture change effort (as opposed to just an opening salvo). They can grow disenchanted when they realize the real hard work is yet to begin. This kind of "leader whiplash" can derail the quick win.

Beware of Employee Backlash

Employees can also be lulled into thinking quick wins are the real deal. Giving them a popular "freebie" (a service or other process improvement they have wanted for a while) can set up false expectations that many more freebies are on the way, an inaccurate perspective on the real purpose of the change effort. They may also think cosmetics are all that is required and will then be disappointed when those minor improvements do not create the major, substantive change they were hoping for.

Culture change is always harder than organizations (and their leaders) predict; it always takes longer than expected. The only antidote to this natural reaction to dissonance is to go the extra mile in communicating with employees— explaining why the change is necessary, giving people an opportunity to air their views and pose questions in town hall-like meetings, and stressing the long-term nature of true cultural transformation. While data overload is rarely a useful endeavor, the wise organization should err on the side of too much information. *Extraordinary* communication is the approach we find most effective throughout the change initiative and especially with the quick-wins element.

Tie Quick Wins to the Major Change Effort

Communication is vital to help employees see how the quick wins fit in with the major change effort. Help employees stay connected to the broader change initiative by communicating and reinforcing these things:

- What you are actually working on: Define the business problem in specific terms.
- Why you selected these initiatives as a part of quick wins: Show a clear linkage to the major change effort.
- Who is involved in the quick-wins effort.
- When the projects or efforts will be completed.
- What will be the specific benefits of the quick wins to customers and employees.

Quick wins are of greatest value during the first two years of a change effort. When utilized effectively, they can tie together various elements of a service plan to actually deliver improved service experiences to customers and employees. Many organizations find during periods of rapid growth that organization charts quickly become obsolete. Customers and employees need to know who to contact to solve service issues, or they face the dreaded "It's not my job but I'll transfer you to Bob." Inevitably, Bob cannot solve the issue either, and another transfer is necessary. These ease-of-accessibility projects provide service improvement to customers by getting them quickly to the person who can best resolve their issue quickly. They also serve to improve internal partnering by improving employee understanding of unit as well as individual roles and responsibilities.

Make Quick Wins a Permanent Fixture of Your Culture

Although many organizations believe quick wins are only of value during the embryonic stages of a change process, they should become a permanent part of the culture. By repeatedly seeking out, executing, and celebrating quick wins, organizations encourage employees to take the initiative in continually searching for and developing ideas for boosting customer service.

As customer expectations change, so too will their demands on your unit or organization. Use the quick-wins effort as a way to keep up with the ever-increasing speed of change in business as well as to keep your organization nimble in responding to customers' new expectations, hopes, and aspirations.

How to Start Quick Wins

Here's a proven way to start quick wins: Put together a cross-functional team (without any of your direct reports) and discuss what service vision–aligned changes the team would recommend—changes that could be implemented in the next thirty days—to clearly communicate to everyone that the service excellence effort is definitely underway. Next ask a group of your most trusted customers and/or vendors what changes the unit or organization should make to create a world-class level of customer service. These three groups should provide more than enough information and ideas to develop an initial list of quick wins. Then it is a matter of selecting the most promising quick-win initiatives from the bunch, determining the appropriate timing, and assigning resources and accountability for each.

A "QUICK WINS" PRIMER

Is the quick win (QW) doable in less than six months?

Is the QW one that employees would say is important to improving the customer's experience?

Is the QW one that employees would view as valuable—something that makes them pleased, makes their work lives easier, or provides encouragement?

Is the QW one that employees would likely see as tangible evidence of leadership's commitment to improving the customer's experience?

Can the QW be communicated in concert with another positive, big event?

Can the results of the QW be sustained, not just become a "flash-in-the-pan," one-time tactic?

Is the QW clearly aligned and in sync with the service vision?

Is the QW one that will create an effect or outcome that would likely be noticed by customers?

Is the QW one that will create an effect or outcome that would likely be valued by customers and make them more committed to the organization?

People don't resist change; they resist the prediction of pain over which they have no control. While getting employees involved in the change process allows them to share control (thus minimizing their resistance), some will never "get it." Sometimes they have such a large emotional investment in the old ways that to relinquish them would be a blow to their pride. This means that some people will not survive the change. In fact, one way employees gauge the real commitment of leadership to change is to test its tolerance for retaining employees who, despite resources and energy devoted to helping them adjust to the change, persist in continuing their old ways. Culture change always requires difficult, but necessary, human resource decisions.

Quick wins are invaluable tools for transforming "here we go again" attitudes into "count me in." Their magic comes from an ability to bridge an exciting start to a necessary tedium, to create a natural transition from the rapid pace of new beginnings to the slow tempo of steady transformation.

18

Craft "Happy" Processes

"You can take great people, highly
trained and motivated, and put them
in a lousy system and the system will
win every time."

—GEARY RUMMLER, CEO
Performance Design Lab

The Native Americans believe that every creation has a soul. Thus, they believe that an inanimate object such as a tree or a rock possesses a spirit just as a horse, bird, or human being does. Organizations that create passionately devoted customers look at their service processes in a similar way. While they know, of course, that an order entry process is not alive, thinking of it in that fashion—as a living, feeling, organic system—helps ensure it is designed and maintained in a way that best serves the organizational "tribe" of customers and employees.

A "live" perspective ensures key service processes receive the proper care and feeding so they don't fall into disrepair and so they consistently deliver the kind of hassle-free, friendly service experiences that create distinction in the market.

Service Processes Defined

Service processes can be defined from two perspectives. From the inside of the organization looking out, they are a collection of procedures and practices that constitute and govern a complete service system. From the outside looking in—the customer's perspective—processes are the steps (and sometimes hoops) companies put customers through to get the products or services they need.

A hotel has a process for check-in. While the operation (check-in) from the customer's perspective might start when he or she approaches the front desk and end with room check-out, for the hotel the process might start with reservations or someone alerting the front desk the hotel was overbooked. And it might not end until the night audit has done an operational review and balanced the shift. There are many process steps invisible to customers that need to be well designed and executed to ensure good end-to-end service experiences.

Cumbersome service processes are the bane of customer loyalty. Most customers would prefer to simply snap their fingers and instantly get the product or outcome they desire. Of course, we can imagine some masochistic customers who simply can't get enough bureaucracy, irritating paperwork, or exasperating delays ("I only stopped by to see if you had some more forms I could fill out" or "I called for one reason—so you could put me on hold again!").

A process might be governed by a set of procedures (fill out the application in triplicate or listen to ten voice-response-unit options before making a choice); a collection of regulations (complete in one hour and provide a copy to security); or even certain laws (enter into the company ledger). But while the primary role of processes is to ensure service is delivered in a consistent and efficient fashion, there is no bylaw stating they should also make customers want to pull their hair out.

How to Make a Process "Happy"

The term "happy process" originated with one of our international clients. We were grappling for a way to explain the meaning of process alignment as a part of developing company-wide service standards and norms. Our client thought about the end result and suggested that one outcome of alignment might be "happy processes"—procedures and practices designed in a way that create unexpected joy for customers and employees because of their simplicity, or ease of use, as viewed through the customer's eyes. Think also of what would make a process happy if it could come alive—it would work well, it would make a difference, and it would gain the admiration of its caretaker. The label proved to be a powerful metaphor that helped employees understand the desired outcome of a company-wide process alignment effort.

There are a number of principles for creating happy processes. Remember, a happy process works hard for everyone—the customer, employees, leaders, the organization, as well as its fellow processes. Following are seven principles for service process happiness management.

#1: Processes must be viewed from the customers' perspective

The customers' perspective trumps processes built for internal convenience every time. A financial services client of ours was going through the first steps in developing service standards when the CEO heard about the excessive wait times customers were experiencing due to limited levels of authority mandated for branch employees. No one was certain when and/or why these levels of authority existed, other than they had been around a long time. When questioned, they were always deemed as "necessary" or "convenient" for organizational risk management purposes.

The CEO set about making immediate changes to improve the customers' experience while still maintaining an appropriate level of risk management. He selected a small group to meet with him the day they returned from their off-site, examined the necessity of the policies, and was able to initiate revised policies that improved the customers' experience (such as reduced customer wait time) while empowering certain employees with more authority. Appropriate risk controls for the firm were maintained.

#2: Processes must be in sync with the organization's service vision

If the service vision is about "customer comfort," then every process must be crafted to facilitate customer comfort. Processes must also always defer to the organization's core values and service standards. Values and standards take precedence over processes and procedures. The organization's service vision, values, and standards should serve as filters that processes are tested against to ensure they are aligned with what is most important to the organization. If speed of service delivery is a key customer loyalty driver and is reflected in the service vision and a standard, then the organization's processes need to stand up to a test of "speed of service"—using the customers' definition of speed.

#3: Processes must facilitate great internal service, not just external service

The creation of silos and shaky handoffs between internal departments hurt process "morale." Silos can be real or just an attitude. In either case, they are a barrier to great service because they prevent the smooth transition of customers (internal and external) and/or issues that impact customers between steps in a process. In the case of a tie, external service trumps internal service. In other words, when designing a new process (or reviewing a process for alignment), the needs and perceptions of the external customer should be viewed as a priority over the desires for ease and efficiency of the internal customer.

#4: Process changes driven by economics must be scrutinized for their impact on customers

Too often, organizations evaluate the economics of process change solely on the return on investment (ROI) in the process change itself without attaching value to the impact the change may have on customers. This is especially true if the impact on customer loyalty will most likely be negative. For example, enterprise resource planning (ERP) initiatives too often are evaluated almost entirely on the basis of the cost of technology and change management without a careful analysis of their impact on customer loyalty. The result is a loud cry from customers about substandard service *after implementation,* which unfortunately causes customer loyalty to drop.

#5: Processes must be regularly updated to reflect customers' expectations

The top ten most important processes—those deemed to have the biggest impact on customer loyalty—must be singled out annually for an alignment check and tune-up. Today, customer expectations change at supersonic speed as customers are influenced by their service experiences with organizations of every type and effectiveness. Staying in touch with these ever-changing customer service expectations is crucial to an organization's success. Just as you would expect a complete check-up from your doctor during an annual physical, so too should your most important processes undergo the rigors of an annual evaluation of their effectiveness at delivering or enabling service to customers in an appropriate fashion.

#6: Inefficient processes must be quickly eliminated

Processes that have been in place for an extended period tend to become overly respected and can become thought of as "untouchable." We are reminded of a client who failed to pay attention to how difficult it was for customers to connect with employees via telephone until one day they were jolted into awareness by a potentially very large referral source for new business. To our client's horror, the potential source described his ridiculously complex journey through an anti-quated VRU (voice response unit) portion of the telephone system and his complete frustration in being unable to find a way through the maze to a real person.

The organization immediately gathered a group of senior leaders and took them on a similar journey via speakerphone. Their embarrassment and irritation grew as they played the role of customer and became increasingly frustrated at the hurdles they had created for their customers in trying to reach their very talented employees. The VRU programming, which had been effective when implemented, had grown stale and become a very large irritant to customers. An annual check-up and realignment of processes could have prevented the occurrence of this situation.

#7: Processes are never completely "happy" unless they are employee-friendly

Leaders are responsible for the "morale" of processes, not the process's custodian or owner. Research has shown that engaged and loyal employees are needed to drive the type of service that produces loyal customers. Just as you would use filters to ensure processes reflect the organization's service vision, so too should you use employee engagement as a filter for testing a process's impact on the employees who are affected by it. We know that executive leaders closely monitor an organization's customer service dashboard for indications of fluctuations in customer loyalty. They also must review customer intelligence for evidence of fluctuations in the alignment of processes.

When the intelligence indicates the need for a process review or redesign, it is leadership's responsibility to implement such an initiative. The process owner's role is to ensure the process is working exactly as designed. Often, process custodians will sense the first signs of unhappiness in a process because they are so close to daily operations. They may sound the alarm of a process entering the realm of misalignment, but it is leadership's responsibility to ensure any adjustments necessary for realignment are in fact realized. If process morale is left to the process custodian, her closeness to the process will prevent her from seeing that change is required.

The Sounds of a Happy Process

The sounds of nature carry a spiritual value for Native Americans. The wind in the trees, the noise of the cricket, and the howl of the distant coyote all form a language that fosters understanding and appreciation. What if you were to interview a really happy process? Let's listen in on part of a recent interview we conducted with the checking account process (CAP) at a large bank. As you review the transcript of the conversation, ask yourself this: If it were possible to interview our own service processes, what insights might we glean that could help us create better or less troublesome experiences for customers or employees?

US   We know what you do, CAP, but who would you say you are?

CAP   Well, I've been called a lot of names! Actually, it depends on whom you talk with. To my customer, I consider myself a conduit. You know, like the electrical wires in your home. I'm not the power—that's the customer's funds. I just help them get the power. But to the bank I'm a "counter." I help management keep track of how much money is in the bank so they can invest it or lend it out. I also secretly work for the FDIC, but we won't talk about that!

US   I realize it's different strokes for different folks . . . or, should I say different payments for different processes . . . but, what turns you on? What makes you happy?

CAP   Oh, that's easy. It's when I see customers with that really confident, secure look on their faces—like I worked for them just exactly like they hoped I would.

US   Let's talk more about that.

CAP   Well, when I'm truly taken care of, I'm almost invisible to customers; everything works like clockwork. It means there's a standard way of doing what I do and everybody remembers what it is. But there's another way it happens. This bank is all about "impeccable accuracy." When the employees who use me remember and are guided by that mantra, I get to do my job in a very special way.

US   Okay, CAP, what else makes you a super happy process?

CAP   You know that I don't work alone here. Customers who use me also use an ATM card and sometimes have direct payment or deposit processes. Some have loans and a savings account. It means I have to get along with other bank processes. What makes me happy is when my caretaker, the bank, helps me to talk with these processes. We're all pretty cooperative if we get to speak the same language.

US   What's the one thing that stresses you the most?

CAP   It's when the bank thinks I am here for its benefit only. I can guarantee you when that happens—and it happened to me with my last caretaker—customers get pretty angry. And they blame me for it!

What does this conversation with CAP teach us? That customer loyalty isn't possible without corporate standards, norms, *and* processes that are all aligned with the service vision. If processes are designed only for internal convenience and not for the customer's benefit—if it's impossible to track down live help in voicemail menus, get service problems resolved without multiple callbacks or hand-offs to other employees, or find what you need quickly and efficiently on e-commerce sites—then those processes are working at cross-purposes with your service vision.

CAP also told us that customers relish reliability—that is, they want assurances that experiences will go as well or better than they expect, each and every time, without any surprises. When all service processes are "happy" and aligned with the vision, it builds trust that bolsters customer confidence . . . and from confidence and trust spring loyalty and strong word of mouth.

Process improvement and process alignment also play crucial roles in culture change efforts. As employees attempt change, they find themselves plowing new ground. This uncertainty causes people to look for assurances that their pioneering efforts are relevant and valued. A major source of that solace comes from evidence that leadership is committed to the change. If employees find themselves continuing to use the same old processes and procedures, it signals that the change is only lip service. They will likely dismiss the change effort as cosmetic and operate as they always have.

The secret to maintaining processes in a state of happiness is to remember they are means, not ends. They are the ultimate servants in the quest for customer loyalty and devotion. Treating them as common slaves will only result in process acquiescence and ultimately customer distain. But treating them as contributing partners will yield process alignment and customer devotion.

Ten Steps to Creating Happy Processes

Still not sure about how to create happy processes? Here's a summary of the process to follow for achieving just that:

1. Determine the most critical business practices, processes, systems, and policies based on the significance of their impact on employee quality of life, customer loyalty, and/or profitability.
2. Identify key alignment filters (key customer loyalty drivers, the service vision, standards and norms, critical strategic building blocks, and so on) to use in testing the critical business practices to determine which ones are out of alignment.
3. Using these alignment filters, develop a list of processes that need adjustment to become realigned.

4. Make sure the realignment list is all-encompassing by comparing it to five service or system breakdowns you were involved in or know of over the past twenty-four months. What company-wide business practices, processes, systems, procedures, and policies, in place at the time, were ineffective in preventing these breakdowns? Review to make sure that all of the latter are on your realignment list.

5. Develop criteria for prioritizing the list of out-of-alignment business practices, processes, systems, procedures, and policies. Consider criteria such as quick wins, "can't wait," major customer impact, and major employee impact to identify the top-ten priorities to work on first.

6. Compare the top-ten priorities to a list of exclusion criteria, such as "Don't have the resources this year," "Already being worked on," or "Have to wait for the new ERP system implementation" to determine which priorities need to come off the list.

7. Identify alignment project executive sponsors, an alignment project leader, and an alignment project "steering committee" to offer guidance, direction, and resources as well as eliminate barriers to success.

8. Assign project team members and develop project plans.

9. Communicate, communicate, communicate about the project, progress, and plans.

10. Celebrate the milestone accomplishments and successes of the alignment project.

19
Devise a Service Dashboard

> "'Tain't nowhere near right, but it's
> approximately correct."
>
> —HOWLAND OWL
> (the Quality Guru of the *Pogo* comic
> strip, explaining the inbred weaknesses
> of all measurement systems)

The stakes for ignoring the "dashboard" of a company—the array of metrics that help monitor and maintain service excellence—are high. Dashboards are vital tools for alerting you to problems, needed alteration and maintenance, as well as necessary course corrections within your service organization. As such, they provide a critical guidance system needed to traverse the marketplace. Just as the odometer of a vehicle alerts you to change the oil or the speedometer warns you to slow down, various components of the organization's dashboard provide myriad information that is key to the organization's progress and success.

The Customer Service Guidance System

Customer service metrics serve different purposes. Course metrics communicate information related to direction and progress. Correction metrics inform ways to alter direction or improve progress. Caution metrics function as an early warning system on potential threats or obstacles that lie ahead. Context metrics help educate the organization on the atmosphere in which the enterprise is operating. If the dashboard were a team of special guides, the course metrics would be called the Pathfinder, correction metrics would be the Adjustor, caution metrics would be the Scout, and the context metrics would be the Weatherman. All these guides must work together to provide a comprehensive guidance system.

Metrics not only serve different purposes, they come in different types. A metric can be quantitative (like the temperature gauge that reads 212 degrees Fahrenheit), qualitative (like steam bellowing from beneath the radiator cap), or inductive. Inductive metrics are largely intuitive conclusions based on seemingly unrelated data. A professional racecar driver would not need the gauge or steam to sense that all was not right with the radiator. Inductive measures are the most advanced type of metric, as well as the most controversial.

Combining metric *purposes* with metric *types* yields a practical 3×4 matrix that can help ensure an organization is gathering service information in a comprehensive fashion. The following illustration of the dashboard of a passenger vehicle shows the interaction of function with type.

THE DASHBOARD OF A PASSENGER VEHICLE

	COURSE	CORRECTION	CAUTION	CONTEXT
Quantitative	Distance to final destination	Speedometer reads: Very fast	GPS indicating a dirt road ahead	External thermometer
Qualitative	Passenger with a new map	Strange knock in the engine	Road advisory from AAA	Deep snow on the roadside
Inductive	Noisy but experienced backseat driver	Previous trouble with engine knocks	No other vehicles coming from the direction traveled	Experience with similar terrain elsewhere

Course—The Metrics for Direction

The first set of metrics includes tools to provide evidence that the organization is "on course," that is, pursuing the direction intended. Think of these metrics as serving a pathfinder role—ensuring you are on the proper trail heading in the proper direction. Organizations use macro metrics like net income, earnings per share, or market share for financial course metrics. A professional sports team might use the number of games won, annual attendance, concessions collected, and product endorsements acquired. If the metric was on the dashboard of a car, it would be telling us we are heading northwest, 10 miles from our destination, and getting 20 miles per gallon.

Course metrics focus largely on outcomes, effects, or results. They are those directly tied to the goals and objectives of the organization. Typically they relate to growth, improvement, and accomplishment. They are the quantification of the critical success factors for the life of the enterprise. Since, in the words of Peter Drucker, "The purpose of an organization is to create and retain customers," course metrics must also cover service performance.

Customer course metrics can be quantitative, like the number of customers retained, the customer's lifetime value, or profits per customer. All this information helps gauge growth and improvement. Qualitative customer course metrics could be anecdotal comments from customers that communicated progress ("My neighbor said I should give you a try") or improvement ("Glad to see you finally got a friendly receptionist"). Inductive measures might include comments from front-line employees, like "Customers don't seem as enthusiastic as they once were."

Correction—The Metrics for Maintenance

The second set of metrics includes tools to better adjust progress and maintain effectiveness. Correction metrics play the adjustor role, providing information to get back on the right track if you're temporarily derailed. These are the means by which an organization gains a deeper and more complete understanding of a course metric. Correction metrics enable an organization to alter direction, change strategy, or do preventive maintenance on some part of the company. This type of metric focuses on the processes, means, or cause. As the course metrics are *outcome* measures, correction metrics are *diagnostic* measures.

If a basketball team was losing games (a course metric), the coach might examine correction metrics such as the number of points gained per particular tactic or play, time of ball possession by each player, or percentage of shots made from certain areas of the floor. The measures might lead a coach to conclude that certain players need to pass the ball more, the team needs to improve accuracy at the foul line, or the team is underutilizing a full-court press when within four points of the opposing team. Correction metrics *enable* performance as course metrics *affirm* performance.

Quantitative customer correction metrics might include customer retention by particular demographic segment or product type, customer satisfaction scores by type of customer, length of customer relationship, or "share of wallet" by segment. Qualitative customer correction metrics would be types of customer complaints, types of errors that trigger refunds, correlations between customer satisfaction scores and some demographic figure, or reasons customers give for leaving the organization. Inductive customer correction metrics might include anecdotal information that the customer does *not* provide that might otherwise be expected (such as the customer who closes a bank account yet isn't moving).

Identifying the right correction metrics starts with a complete dissection of the course metrics. For example, if a key course metric is the number of customers under age twenty-five who re-enroll in a program after one year, the correction metrics might be derived from interviews with those who stay versus those who leave to find out the predominant reasons for both. If the number-one reason given for customer turnover is the lack of communication from the organization acknowledging the customer when they sign up for a second year, the correction metric might be the number of customer visits made by employees within sixty days prior to enrollment. Every course metric is comprised of many correction metrics. The goal is to have enough to be comprehensive but not so many as to be unmanageable.

Caution—The Metrics for Early Warning

The third set of metrics includes tools to provide information (a.k.a., intelligence) needed to proactively shape or change direction or to respond defensively to the competition. Just like the scout out in front of the fort or flank of soldiers, this is the data vital to effective early warning. The athletic team mentioned earlier might look at next year's schedule, scouting reports, or an announcement that a key opponent just recruited a renowned offensive coach. A car, for example, might include quantitative information like the odometer reading since the last radiator overhaul, qualitative data like the long-range weather report, or inductive information like whether the dog's fur is thicker than last year, indicating a particularly cold winter ahead.

Quantitative customer caution metrics might be those associated with long-range demographic variations, industry projections, and anticipated psychographic changes in a target population. Qualitative customer caution metrics could be results from pilots, focus groups, industry predictions, and futuring studies. Inductive customer caution metrics might be the advice of long-term employees who have witnessed trends and the organization's reaction to them or the hunches drawn from comparing projected demographics with predicted psychographics. Customer caution metrics are by definition tentative and predictive.

Context—The Metrics for the Marketplace

The final set of metrics includes the tools to better understand the setting or marketplace and where the unit or organization stands relative to that milieu. Like the weatherman who delivers information that helps you plan apparel or rearrange future plans, context metrics teach you about the broader environment in which you operate. Putting a car through its paces on a hot day will have a completely different impact on the radiator than the same actions in the dead of winter. Understanding the marketplace and competitors' strategies is crucial to success, since no organization performs in a vacuum.

Quantitative customer metrics include how similar organizations fare in the same market conditions—same-store customer churn compared to similar companies, or industry standing in revenue per available room or per employee. Qualitative customer metrics might be the number of times the company is favorably mentioned in trade journals, rankings in independent surveys, or recognition from the community, industry, or profession. Inductive customer metrics might be the number of top performers being recruited compared to the competition or employee turnover—and where departing workers find new employment.

Context metrics paint a picture of the particular environment in which the organization is operating at a point in time. Such metrics protect companies against becoming so myopic or inwardly focused that competitive mistakes are made. Think of course metrics as answering the question, "How are we doing relative to our objectives, goals, and mission?" Correction metrics help answer the question, "What variables are keeping us from being on course?" Caution metrics show, "What lies in our path that might impact our course or progress?" And context metrics help answer the question, "How are we doing compared to our competition or other organizations like us with similar challenges?"

Making Your Guides Work as a Team

Using a dashboard has its advantages and limitations. Too many athletic teams have lost games focusing on the scoreboard—particularly when they are ahead in the contest and begin to coast—instead of playing the game. Conversely, there's the case of the novice farmer who completely ignores the dashboard, leading his tractor's radiator to break down. All dashboards are an assortment of measurements and signals. And measurements have principles that govern their effective management. Following are a few principles that can help you mix and match measurements for maximum effectiveness.

#1: Metrics and numbers are not the same

There is a *Saturday Night Live* comedy routine that has the sports announcer giving the ballgame scores without the names of teams, "And now for the basketball scores. 89–75, 92–80, 75–74 . . . here's a halftime score: 45." The spoof dramatizes the pointlessness of calculations without a context.

A metric is a tool used in conjunction with a standard to help measure, monitor, or evaluate. Two key words—tool and standard—tell the tale. A metric is a tool. That means that, in and of itself, it is useless. It requires a skilled and thoughtful handler to harness its power. It is also "used in conjunction with a standard," not in a void. We are impressed when someone scores fifty points in basketball or pitches a no-hitter because, when measured against standards of success in those sports, the achievements are admirable. Without a clear standard on the business end of the metric, it would be as inane as a score without a team.

Metrics are the dashboards of the business world. And numbers are a popular language, especially the closer you get to the executive suite. However, arithmetic does not tell the whole story. As reassuring as irrefutable numbers might be, qualitative information may be more helpful. The patient who reports a very sore throat, severe headaches, and ringing in the ears may be telling the physician much more useful information than the numbers the doctor reads on the thermometer or blood-pressure gauge. Be careful of an infatuation with numbers. It may seduce you into ignoring the standard, forgetting the context, and misusing the tool.

#2: Don't use a ruler to measure your temperature

Measurement management includes the selection of the right tools. Just like those that grace automobiles, effective service dashboards are comprised of a variety of types of metrics. We use pounds per square inch and tread depth to determine if a tire is in working order, weight and quarts to measure the right viscosity and quantity of oil. To say we have fifteen gallons of air in the car tires would be interesting, but pointless.

Measurement selection starts with a careful identification of the critical success factors of an organization. The movement in corporate accounting from net earnings to EBITDA (earnings before interest, taxes, depreciation, and amortization) is a positive example of selecting a tool that reflects the type of earnings line managers can directly influence. Seventy-five percent of customers who leave organizations for competitors mark themselves as "completely satisfied" on surveys; satisfaction, it seems, doesn't equate to loyalty. Therefore, customer service metrics that monitor satisfaction (rather than customer loyalty) lull the organization into thinking it is giving great service when it may be only giving adequate service.

The dashboard is meaningless if it measures the wrong items. Begin with measurements of key service quality features that the *customer* deems important. One company we know of was responsible for delivering its customers' equipment all over the country on a very timely basis; leadership's focus had been on order accuracy and ensuring equipment wasn't damaged in transit. However, a customer service survey revealed that for customers, on-time delivery was also crucial. With that feedback in hand, the company shifted from focusing solely on order accuracy and safe shipping to a dashboard metric that measured timely delivery of equipment. Critical success factors mean "critical," not "nice to have."

#3: When the only tool you have is a hammer, all problems look like nails

That famous line from Abraham Maslow captures the essence of another measurement management issue: inappropriately overusing a favorite metric. "Bottom line results" is a metric too often used to inappropriately justify, add, or exclude countless valuable efforts. But as one executive said, "If every decision was made on the basis of solid, quantifiable numbers, you could hire a data clerk to be CEO." The most important organizational decisions often rely on a thoughtfully considered leap of faith.

All-important gauges don't measure cause and effect. Dramatically increasing customer loyalty is not guaranteed to increase profits if your core customer base is too small, the store is in the wrong location, and purchasing is paying too much for inventory. As much as customer service gurus would like to promise cause and effect, there are typically more variables in the profit mix than customer evaluation.

#4: Anything not worth measuring is not worth measuring well

Gathering data to transform into metrics can be laborious. It is important to be selective and to only make data as precise as is needed to achieve the purpose. Calibrating each dial to cover every conceivable contingency not only creates data overload, it leads to "working the math and missing the point." Keep in mind that metrics are tools—a working language that paints a picture or tells a story. It is the picture or story that becomes a call to action, not the math.

A bank found a strong relationship between teller turnover and customer satisfaction among branch customers. The correlation was not surprising—customers did not like having to "train" a new (and slower) person on their particular banking habits, needs, and requirements. But instead of working to decrease turnover of key employees, the bank turned its energy to gathering even more precise information on what things turnover impacted. The result was reams of irrelevant information and delayed implementation of a correction to the problem.

#5: *Metrics belong on the wall, not in a three-ring binder*

Dashboards should have maximum impact on the way we do business. For that to happen, information should be easily accessible and/or widely disseminated throughout the company. Too often senior management puts the dashboard metrics under lock and key, rendering it unavailable to employees on the front line. In other cases the marketing department is asked to create a sanitized version of results. The rationale for the hoarding or selective release of performance data is often to "keep competitors out of the info," but the effect is to rob employees closest to customers of timely information needed to maximize customer service.

Wise organizations sacrifice measurement purity for feedback urgency. They know that 80 percent of the data now is better than 100 percent of the data later. In the fast-paced, ever-changing marketplace in which organizations operate today, real time not only means quickly, it means "real," as in authentic and raw.

Keep Your Eye on the Road, Not the Dashboard

Racing great Dale Earnhardt once told a group of admirers, "Racing is way too hectic to watch a bunch of dials. If you don't keep it simple, you'll be watching RPMs and misread the track. I count on my crew to mind the details." Managing an organization in today's economy is a lot like driving a racecar. You not only need the right metrics, you need the right *number* of metrics. And you rely on your crew to go to school on data sliced and diced myriad ways to support its recommendations. Provide the "crew" all of the metrics it needs to maximize its performance. Leadership needs top-line data only.

Once the appropriate metrics have been selected, refined, and communicated, it is vital they become a part of the portfolio of leadership tools. Just as metrics such as sales volume, earnings per share, and net operating costs are tools leaders use for financial guidance, customer service metrics must become an equally valued device for effective leadership. Great leadership is about worrying more about the road ahead than the dashboard. The following are some principles to keep in mind.

Avoid expecting "A" while measuring "B"

We live in a world enamored with metrics. "What gets measured gets done" is more often true than not. The good news is that metrics lend discipline to the operation of the enterprise; the bad news is that unmanaged metrics can yield unintended results. Senior management in one company introduced an exciting new product at an annual big-deal sales rally. Leaders were confident the hype would motivate salespeople to promote the new product. Six months later new product sales were dismal. A closer look revealed the cause. The commission to salespeople for selling the new product was no different than the commission to promote the old but "familiar" product line. In the sales world, behavior usually follows incentives.

Customer service metrics can take on a life of their own, far from the intent of leadership, unless they are aligned with an organization's key business practices, policies, processes, and systems. If the customer service dashboard is to provide relevant guidance information, it will need to be anchored to the organization's mission statement, service vision, and corporate standards, and the scorecards should be used for performance management and compensation. Review metrics frequently to make sure what is being measured is what is really important to customers—those performance areas that have the biggest influence on their loyalty, not just their satisfaction.

Avoid expecting "A" while measuring everything but "A"

All leaders believe in delivering great customer service. Many mouth the platitude, "Take care of the customer and the customer will take care of you." Most corporate mission statements contain a reference to the importance of the customer. Yet take a close look at the typical executive management scorecard. Somehow, the call imploring a "passion for customers" is rarely converted into a key criterion for success.

Try this. Assume your organization uses a survey that asks customers to rate overall service satisfaction on a 1 to 5 scale. Last year the overall average customer rating was a 4. But this year it dropped to a 3. What would be the consequence to executive management? Would leaders be demoted, replaced, or deprived of bonuses? Would the drop trigger significant organizational changes? Not likely, right?

Now, take the same example but with one change. Instead of the 1 to 5 scale being a measure of customer satisfaction, assume it was profits measured in millions (or billions)—that is, your last year's profit of $4 million dropped to $3 million. Same question, what would be the consequence to executive management? If customer service is as important as the hallway banners and annual report claims it is, metrics in that area must be given the same weight and consequence as other measures dissected and discussed over the boardroom table.

Include metrics for monitoring service to colleagues
One often-overlooked factor important to overall service excellence is the relationship between internal and external customer service excellence. Countless research studies have shown a direct correlation between the quality of internal service—how coworkers service each other—and the service

delivered to external customers. A truly effective customer service dashboard will include several measures of internal service to colleagues.

When formulating a list of metrics to be included on the dashboard, ask this question: Does the organization have clear service standards, practices, policies, and procedures that promote partnership *between and among* units, not just good teamwork *within* units? Absent any cross-unit service metrics, it is difficult for leaders to get early warning on the emergence of silo thinking or any brewing turf battles. Inter-unit collaboration is essential to the kind of seamless service that creates loyal customers.

Dashboards are only one part of a guidance system

The customer service dashboard is only one part of a larger guidance system that includes a strategic plan, financial plan (budget), corporate standards, service vision, behavioral norms, performance objectives, and many other tools that enable the organization to effectively compete in its marketplace. Keep the dashboard in perspective as a tool.

As one piece of a larger guidance system pie, the customer service dashboard must be in sync with other navigational tools. While being anchored to up-to-date customer needs and requirements is sacrosanct, being aligned with the organization's vision is equally crucial. It is important that the elements that make up the dashboard be periodically reviewed to ensure what is used is relevant and fits with the rest of the guidance system. Will the dashboard metric assess the company's success as defined in the strategic plan? Will a metric measure performance aligned with core values? Will a measure assist in monitoring the customer's experience to see how closely it matches the company's vision for that experience?

Make metrics your one-a-day vitamin

Once proposed, dashboard metrics have to be tested to ensure they can become relevant anchors; it's important they become integrated and embedded into the organization's culture. As with any culture change effort, leadership will need to be actively involved and to serve as role models of how to successfully integrate the metrics. This is not an endeavor that can be delegated to a project team. Ask yourself this: What organization would turn over responsibility for crafting a corporate strategic plan to a project team? Leadership attention spells "priority" to those skeptical employees looking for signs the new effort is just another passing fad.

Dashboard rollout should include easy access to the metrics and training on how to understand and use them. The dashboard should also become part of the guidance system for recruiting, selection, training, promotion, and performance management. Data generated by dashboard metrics can be used to inform and enhance decision-making in all of those talent management subsystems. Last but far from least, true alignment comes when leadership measures and rewards performance on the exact same basis as that measured by the customer service dashboard.

20
Promote Partnerships

"When spider webs unite, they can tie
up a lion."

—ETHIOPIAN PROVERB

When Tom was a little boy, television was the impetus
for much of his backyard play. He and his friends
would watch *Batman and Robin* and then race to the
backyard to reenact what they'd seen on the show.
After what seemed like an hour of arguing over who
would be the "masked warrior," they would settle in to
subdue the evil forces with their toy guns and make-
shift Batmobile. Whether cowboys and Indians, cops
and robbers, or pitchers and batters, television shows
inspired much of Tom's recreational activity.

Tom is now the CEO of a major high-tech company. However, TV still influences his thinking. His
company had recently acquired a smaller software
group to bolster its information technology (IT)
capacity and provide more responsive sales support.
The merger had been rocky and Tom was extremely

frustrated about in-fighting between the operations and sales departments. Customer complaints were climbing, field salespeople were frustrated, and the new software enhancements the acquired company was supposed to produce were still stuck in applications development.

"I'm getting sick and tired of the silos," Tom snapped as he slammed his hand on his desk. "I need better teamwork. Why can't these guys quit arguing in the huddle, just call the play, and get back to basic blocking and tackling?!"

It was the Tuesday morning after a popular televised sports contest. Batman and Robin loomed in the cobwebs of Tom's mind as he considered using lessons from the game he'd just watched to help heal and unite his fractured company. But despite the apparent parallels in situations, the thought caused him to reach for the wrong solution to a common work problem. Tom's problem was not poor teamwork, but rather ineffective partnering.

Partnering is the critical success factor for all relationships in today's world of enterprise. A partnership might be a relationship between an external supplier and a company, between two internal divisions in an organization, or an affiliation of two companies joining forces to create a breakthrough product. These alliances act very differently than teams. Their rise and fall is based far less on the efficacy of their efforts and far more on the success of their synergy. Like strong, enduring marriages, good partnerships prosper because they are based on shared values like respect, honesty, openness, and a desire for win-win solutions. The best partnerships are a form of unconditional serving where the service provider often consciously overlooks short-term costs to lay the foundation of a long-term relationship.

Customer service can and does suffer as a result of poor teamwork or when workers in the same unit fail to communicate, don't cooperate to solve customer problems, or when individuals place their own needs above team goals. But even more customer disappointments result from a lack of partnership. When partnerships are not planted, cultivated, and fertilized, organizational weeds called silos creep in and take control. Silos are about turf protection, isolation, and failure to view the organization as a whole rather than a collection of disjointed parts. People who live in silos are masters of blame, subterfuge, and manipulation. There may be great teamwork within silos, but unless there is great partnership across units, customers will suffer from inconsistency and frequent service breakdown, resulting in a loss of trust and confidence in the organization.

Teamwork Versus Partnership: Key Differences

Despite similarities, teamwork and partnership are, at their core, different animals. Emulating the teamwork of the Dallas Cowboys or Atlanta Falcons *within* the operations department may heighten synergy and collective productivity. But it is the wrong model for how the operations department interacts with the sales department. An intact business unit relies on *teamwork* for success. But different units or entities (whether an external vendor alliance or the relationship with the internal department down the hall) rely on *partnership* for success. Applying teamwork tactics in a partnership context can lead to flawed practices and counter-productive behavior.

Here are a few of the key differences between teams and partnerships:

1. A team is focused on accomplishing individual tasks and marshals all of its resources to that end. A partnership is focused on creating a *relationship context* from which all manner of outcomes can be accomplished. In a team, accomplishing a *task* is preeminent. In a partnership, excellence cannot be sustained without creation of a superior *relationship*, no matter how compelling the mission. A partnership takes the long view, not a transactions-based, "one and done" perspective.

2. A team suspends the individuality of its members in the pursuit of interdependent action. Collaboration (co-laboring) means "two become one" in the way that two horses working in harmony pull a wagon. In fact, teams work to tone down lone wolf behavior in their quest to create a new whole; the focus is on mix or blend (as one would mix yellow with blue to produce green—in green, the individual root colors disappear). In a partnership, individuality remains as important as jointness or union, and the focus is on the amalgamation of different units or entities, not on a comingling.

3. Good leadership is vital to the effectiveness of a team. Generally, a great amount of energy is devoted to leadership enlistment, getting associates to accept, value, and respond to followership induction. Even in leaderless or self-directed teams—those groupings aimed at operating without the formal identification of authority—a sort of pack mentality encourages the emergence of a leader. In partnerships, followership is less person-centered and more spirit centered. Partners follow a spirit or energy that may emanate from a partner but is not owned by that partner. It is that sense of co-ownership that gives the partnership vitality and drive.

Theory into Practice

Knowing the difference between a team and a partnership might win you an academic argument, but how does it help with the high-tech CEO. The implications of these differences are profound. Trying to make a partnership a team is as flawed and problematic as using mules as breeding stock. Following are several key lessons about the difference between teams and partnerships that can help you choose the right tactic for the particular workplace challenge.

Match Values, Not Just Talents

Teams depend principally on complementary talents more than congruent values. Partnerships can overcome a mismatch in capacities if the relationship is grounded in a common vision and congruent values. "We realized we were two left feet early on," says Frank Esposito, CEO of the global power sport aftermarket distributor Tucker-Rocky Distributing, speaking of his company's alliance with a

Taiwanese company on production of a major helmet project. "But because we shared the same values of honesty, fair play, and commitment, we were able to shore up our mismatch before it derailed our effort."

The high-tech CEO we visited earlier asked his two division heads to write down four work values on which they would refuse to compromise. When both divisions discovered that three of their four values were the same, it provided common ground and new energy for collaboration; the units immediately sat about working to accommodate the fourth value that was different. The more sales and operations heads approached the relationship from a perspective of shared values, the more their differences seemed minor or petty.

Nurture Equality, Not Just Synergy

If partnerships are indeed power-free alliances, effort must be devoted to nurturing and bolstering equality. The CEO's troubles with sales and operations were in part caused by their battles over turf, influence, and recognition. Operations did not want sales horning in on its territory; sales did not want operations getting the right to influence certain decisions that sales considered its purview. Power *over* another was the driver, not power *with*.

When the CEO later reassured both groups (in a meeting with representatives from both sides) that turf, influence, and recognition were not relevant or in jeopardy, both sides let go of their tug-of-war to decide who was going to be top dog.

It's not necessary for groups or units to give up their special identity or key goals to partner effectively. Success is more about creating a level playing field and ensuring one partner's priorities don't consistently take precedence over another's. "If our support staff at global headquarters thinks they have to lose their uniqueness in order to effectively partner with the regional staff in the field, they lose the fruitfulness of their diversity," said Steve Joyce, senior vice president of Strategic Alliances for Marriott International. "The reverse is equally true."

Negotiate Covenants, Not Just Objectives

Partnerships work because the relationships are anchored to a set of informal covenants or agreements specific to the relationship. Teams may learn lessons from some fun-filled ropes-and-ladders courses, but partnerships are spawned from covenants that guide values and behavior, not just outcomes and results.

Value Early Warning Mechanisms

Partnerships are *purposeful* relationships—success hangs on a perpetual focus on their mutual purpose or vision. Maintenance of the relationship—ensuring both sides feel valued and are receiving outcomes they seek—is considered as vital as the clarity of direction. Great partners establish "cues" or early warning mechanisms that signal hiccups in the relationship, allowing both sides to come together to address problems before they mushroom and damage a partnership beyond repair.

Every partnership experiences strains triggered by change, be it price changes, downsizing, acquisition, or uncontrollable factors like an economic downturn. Too often partners take the see-no-evil approach to ignore intuitive signs of problems in the making. But in the best partnerships, feedback is seen as nurturance rather than critique; advice is valued as supportive instruction rather than coercive superiority. A key question our high-tech CEO asked both sales and operations units was this: "How much time elapses between when your gut tells you there's tension in the relationship and when your partner hears you talk about that tension?" When both divisions agreed to work toward a zero time lapse, assumptions were quickly clarified and innuendos were traded in for frankness. Vision gives partnerships direction and covenants give them boundaries. Cues serve as scouts on the lookout for hiccups in the making.

Making Silos Disappear

Silos are the nemesis of customer loyalty. When partners aren't working as one to serve customers—when there aren't seamless hand-offs between internal departments in resolving customer complaints or a spirit of cross-unit cooperation is lacking—it's the customer who often bears the brunt. Silos are eliminated by focusing on collective goals, not territorial gains, and by leaders championing and rewarding cooperation, not derisive competition.

Consider the difference between how lions and wild dogs hunt prey. Lions come together only for the hunt, but as soon as a gazelle or other prey is subdued, they fight among themselves for the spoils. Wild dogs function as a partnership before, during, and after the hunt. They are careful to make certain every member of the pack gets its fair share. The result? A pride of lions is only successful in subduing its prey 20 percent of the time. Wild dogs have an 80 percent success rate, making them the most efficient hunters in the wild. Resolve to make your organization more like the wild dogs than the lions.

Without partnership there is great risk of uneven, non-aligned service experiences. When customers are forced into picking the person, location, or time to ensure they get the service they seek—because any other choice is a crapshoot—their trust erodes and loyalty fades. Consistent, aligned service comes through departments that have great teamwork within the unit and great partnership across units.

Partnerships are instruments of customer trust. They enable the kind of effective collaboration needed for seamless service experiences. They are the catalysts of alignment, that ingredient most crucial to service without drag, dissonance, or disappointment. They are the tools that bring out the best in Loyalty Creators.

Partnerships also require a deeper commitment than more transient service relationships. But they are almost always worth the extra effort. Not only are they more financially rewarding, they can survive more mistakes, are more forgiving over time, and generate greater psychic payoffs than more fleeting and transaction-based business encounters.

COVENANTS FOR COLLABORATION

Great partnerships operate with a clear set of agreements worked out with an obvious commitment to success. Following are a collection of covenants from successful work partnerships:

Negotiate relationship agreements (covenants) regarding communications, trust, and discipline.

Work out ways to provide early feedback (cues) when problems between partners appear to be brewing.

Always assert the truth when behaviors or performance waivers from what was agreed upon.

Keep your promises—or renegotiate them in good faith with ample lead time.

Honor your partner by sharing credit and seeking ways to affirm contributions.

Bring continuous passion and attentive energy to the relationship.

Keep your sights tenaciously on the partnership vision and purpose.

When in doubt, ask, don't assume; when you know, say it.

Assume innocence until guilt is proven.

Encourage an atmosphere of smart risk-taking through trust and unconditional acceptance of each other.

Refuse to let the structure of the organization interfere with good communication with each other. Go directly to the person with whom you need to communicate.

21
Unearth and Nurture Talent

"You start with good people, you train and motivate them, you give them an opportunity to advance—then the organization succeeds."

—J. W. "BILL" MARRIOTT, JR.
Chairman and CEO, Marriott International, Inc.

The number-one impact on customer relations is employee relations. This finding has been consistently reaffirmed across countless research studies. When organizations have energized employees who enthusiastically provide remarkable service, the natural result is a more energized and loyal base of customers.

What causes employees to be energized? Many factors create "turned on" people, but research tells us that how employees are treated by their immediate manager plays a predominant role in their attitude and manner. To be more specific, organizations with an abundance of energized employees delivering remarkable service have leaders that treat them the same way they want employees to treat customers. Why is the leader such a significant influencer of remarkable service? Because employees take most of their cues about how they should serve and treat customers by how leaders talk about and model service behaviors.

Selecting Talent

The leader-employee-customer link starts with selecting talent hard-wired for service—people who have service-oriented attitudes and manners. Customer-centric organizations know that technical skills can be taught, but a desire to serve others, a willingness to engage in repeated customer contact, and a capacity to stay calm when customers lose control are often inbred attributes that must be hired for. Leaders in these organizations take their cues from the likes of Southwest Airlines, where the mantra is "Select for attitude; train for skill."

Selection is not the sole province of human resources; it is a role shared by every employee who comes in contact with a potential employee. We should all be recruiters of great talent, perpetually on the lookout for those who might be assets to our organizations. Once job candidates are identified, it's critical that selection criteria and people-picking processes reflect the new "service attitude" that flows directly from the service vision, standards, and norms.

Unearthing and nurturing talent also includes ensuring new employees are "on boarded" or oriented in ways that make them feel valued and respected, become steeped in the service vision, and are highly trained in technical and interpersonal skills. It also means finding ways to keep people inspired, refreshed, and energized so they can deliver remarkable day-to-day service.

Casting Loyalty Creators

Selecting people for customer service roles is similar to casting people for roles in a play or movie. Both require artful performances aligned with audience expectations. Creating a service experience that customers remember as pleasant or dazzling is like the actor's mission of getting audiences so caught up in the play or movie they start believing the performer is the person portrayed. And like casting for acting roles, success in hiring for service positions depends heavily on finding the right personality fit.

Here are a few tips for casting Loyalty Creators.

#1: Clearly define the service role and the critical qualities you are looking for

The search for potential service stars begins with a clear view of the service role to be filled. First, define the skills the service person must bring and those that can be learned on the job. Then focus on the specific interpersonal qualities—personality, attitudes, and belief systems—that are important. Loyalty Creators have a strong need to serve others, an ability to deal effectively with upset customers without feeling personally affronted, a team spirit, and the creativity and confidence to find unique solutions to customer problems.

#2: Make the casting process match the performance outcome

Years of experience have taught Walt Disney World that one of the most important skills for employees in service roles is the ability to get along well with others. Managers

judge potential cast members—Disney's term for employees—through group interviews. The group experience mir-
rors the contact between cast members and guests. Simulate
customer service requests first, and then advance to more
difficult situations with coworkers or customers.

#3: Gauge the applicant's capacity to create a relationship with the "audience"

From the customer's standpoint, every performance is
"live" and hence unique. It earns the best reviews when it
appears genuine, perhaps even spontaneous. It should never
be rigidly scripted—certainly not canned. The implication
for selection is that super service people must have good per-
son-to-person skills; their speaking, listening, and interacting styles should sound natural and friendly and appropriate
to the situation—neither stiff and formal nor overly familiar.
Watch how applicants treat those around them before, during, and after the interview. Job seekers can teach you a lot
about how they are likely to treat customers by the way they
treat noncustomers.

#4: Test how the applicant reacts to pressure and stress

You don't have to conduct stressful interviews to ascer-
tain stress management skills. Simply asking an applicant to
recall a time when he or she encountered an irate customer
may be adequate. If that doesn't yield good information,
simulating an experience with an irate customer might be
necessary. Be willing to push the encounter issue in order
to have the candidate demonstrate, on the spot, his or her

ability to handle tough situations. Beware of applicants who "love all customers." Choose people who are respectful of and attentive to customers' needs and expectations, not those who are naïve.

On-Boarding Talent

On-boarding, or new employee orientation, starts on day one. It's important that employees become immersed in the culture of service excellence as quickly as possible—and equally important that line leaders play a lead role in delivering the service message. While human resources necessarily plays a broad and crucial role in orientation, the message of service excellence carries more weight with employees if delivered by their managers.

Just as it's vitally important to manage a new customer's initial experience with an organization, it's crucial that employees' first exposure to their new organization be carefully stage-managed. Research shows that how orientation is handled has a big influence on avoidable turnover.

It's helpful to think of orientation as a form of adoption. Adopting a new family member involves a discussion of values, not just tasks; philosophy, not just benefits; customs, not just policies. In the business world, this adoption process serves as a powerful socialization tool that can bolster pride, ensure fit, and help new employees start to build important social networks. Horst Schulze, retired president of the Ritz-Carlton Hotel Company, puts it this way: "There is no more impressionable time in the life of associates than in their first month with a new organization."

One organization took the concept of adoption to a unique level, employing an ADOPT acronym to represent the five steps in its on-boarding process. The following steps are designed to help new hires feel more like "family" than a "foreigner":

Affirm: Provide new employees affirmation they made a wise decision in joining the organization. At the Ritz-Carlton Hotels, it begins with the words, "You are a gift to us."

Debrief: Ask new hires what they've seen in the organization's service operations that may not make sense to them. Remember, new employees are more like customers than seasoned associates. As such, they can see things long-term employees take for granted.

Orient: Help new employees learn the power and importance of the service vision, values, standards, and norms.

Partner: Assign employees a partner for thirty to sixty days to help them learn the informal parts of the culture—those do's and don'ts not found in the policy manual that are typically only learned through painful and sometimes embarrassing trial and error.

Tribe-ready: Think of this Native American ritual as a very positive form of hazing. As initiation helps people feel a part of a club, fraternity, or sorority, tribe-ready activities can be a valuable rite of passage. Assign new employees a task, assignment, or project that benefits the organization and makes people feel they are a valued new addition.

Training Talent

"Learning is the glue that binds together all the pieces of a flourishing culture," wrote Harvard University Professor Rosabeth Moss Kanter. "Leaders of such cultures are more powerful role models when they learn than when they teach." While vision provides an organization with direction and standards provide discipline, leadership ensures it has guidance. Perpetual learning infuses the culture with energy, adaptability, and a future-oriented focus. Cultural transformation works when employees view learning not as a dreaded activity or an escape from daily toil, but as a means to a more productive and fulfilling work life.

When CEO Jack Welch sought to make General Electric the dominant player in its markets, he didn't turn first to his CFO, COO, or CIO. He went first to his chief learning officer, Noel Tichy, knowing that rapid and continuous learning would be the engine to drive and sustain success. Tichy helped turn GE's corporate learning center into an incubator for change, making it one of the most studied and benchmarked training facilities in the country. He also helped Welch develop GE's infamous "work-out" sessions. The concept is based on the premise that those closest to the work know it best, and their brainpower and ideas for improving company operations should be tapped and shared with the rest of the organization.

Tichy would later write in his book, *Control Your Destiny or Someone Else Will*, "Radically altering the genetic code of a large, successful corporation requires revolutionary action.

The work-out sessions served as a tonic in achieving that end."

Training has a number of vital roles in developing a culture of service excellence. It is first and foremost a tool for developing workforce competencies—skills, knowledge, and abilities—that ensure customers get what they expect in the manner they expect it.

It also helps introduce and reinforce behaviors and mindsets central to a new service excellence culture. When people learn with others, they gain collective competence as well as individual confidence. Because training is still primarily a group experience (even with the rise of self-directed e-learning), it can be a crucible for correcting erroneous assumptions about others that erect barriers to partnership and teamwork.

Above all, training must be grounded in a customer-centric philosophy and in sync with the service vision. Without a for-the-customer perspective, new competencies gained will simply promote a focus on tasks or internal efficiencies. If the organizational strategy is to provide remarkable service, then that purpose must be reflected in the way training is planned, designed, and delivered.

It's also imperative that emphasis be placed on transfer of learning. If the new methods or skills learned in training aren't supported back on the job—if their use isn't encouraged by bosses and fortified through opportunities for practice—the skills or knowledge will quickly atrophy.

There are many routes to productive application, but all have one characteristic—integration. The learner's leader should be involved in the learning process before and after attendance. Careful attention must be given to how new and shaky skills are reinforced and supported as they become imbedded in the learner's repertoire of competencies.

Integration includes ensuring training reflects the organization's core values. When there is a disconnect between what is learned in the classroom and what happens in the workplace, new learning is the part that is discarded. An array of tactics should be crafted to ensure learning is integrated with the realities of work and assimilated with the plans for cultural transformation.

Channeling Talent

Channeling talent—guiding, steering, or managing it— cannot effectively happen without accountability. Creating accountability has four dimensions:

1. Ensuring there is a meeting of the minds about what *counts* (performance expectations).
2. Agreeing on how to *count* performance (the means for performance verification).
3. Communicating that "what one can *count* on" is either well on track or in jeopardy of getting off track.
4. Taking a clear-eyed *accounting* of accomplishments and results.

These four pieces—expectations, verification, feedback, and evaluation—form the basis of effective performance management.

Organizations known for great service ensure that discussions of "what counts" are aligned with the service vision, standards, and norms. When Ritz-Carlton Hotel supervisors outline expectations, the echoes of "ladies and gentlemen serving ladies and gentlemen"—a key element of the Ritz service vision—can be symbolically heard in the background. Anchoring expectations to vision and standards helps employees find purpose in their work. It also helps bolster consistency and alignment, essential ingredients in building customer trust.

Discussions around performance are invariably breeding grounds for dissonance and conflict. Think of the last performance appraisal where you received a grade or evaluation much different than you expected or thought you deserved. Your rebuttal (or private thoughts) no doubt wandered into the realm of "how excellence is defined." Your B+ was someone else's C-. Avoiding widely differing interpretations of performance starts with creating upfront clarity and agreement on what types of behaviors or results warrant poor, average, or excellent appraisal ratings.

Channeling is most effective when performance feedback is provided as soon as what is happening is not aligned with what one is counting on. Feedback should be clear, useful, and translatable into new practices targeted at effective performance; the focus should be on improving future behavior, not rebuking past mistakes. The more feedback the better, but at a minimum employees should receive detailed and thoughtful input on their performance once a quarter.

Finally, channeling talent requires appropriate consequences for poor performance, nonperformance, and great performance. Performance management efforts should include discussions of expected versus actual performance as well as plans for improvement and development. Instead of the traditional parental approach to performance review, a more productive method is to ask employees to do the bulk of the premeeting preparation and to present results of past performance, plus plans for future performance, to their supervisors.

The importance of consequences cannot be overstated. For accountability to thrive in an organization there must be consequences, good and bad, appropriate to the performance and delivered fairly and timely throughout the company. If there are clear expectations, accurate verification, frequent feedback to adjust performance as needed, but less than effective performance, there should be consequences. If people regularly make promises they do not keep and are allowed to escape consequences, it signals that poor performance will be tolerated. Not only can that lack of accountability demoralize the organization's strong performers, it can sow the seeds for deterioration in service quality and undermine other organizational results.

The word "talent" is derived from a measure of money (a talent-weight of gold or silver). Students of the Bible know the parable of three servants who were each given different talents; the story's hero is the one who cultivated and made the most of his talent. In the same vein, customer-centric organizations know that the key to their success is identifying, developing, and retaining top service talent. It starts with hiring employees with "proper worth"—those with the attitudes and attributes best suited for an enterprise competing on service excellence. It continues with ensuring that talent is effectively acclimated, trained, guided, and rewarded.

Conclusion

Customer service has been on a roller-coaster ride for the last fifteen years. It was not that long ago the buzzword was "customer satisfaction." Banners, bands, and banter told employees to start focusing on satisfying the customer. After all, the customer was always right. But the customer service bar has been raised. Satisfied customers are fickle. They abandon an organization over the tiniest hiccup, a more convenient location, a change in the front-line server, or just because they want something different. The real service winners today focus on customer loyalty.

The criterion for customer loyalty has also changed. As quality initiatives have impacted product quality, and the globalization of the economy has eliminated competing on price, customers have turned to the quality of their experience as their key determiner of value. Remarkable service is about creating consistently great experiences for customers. Bottom line, it is all about people who serve customers and each other with the philosophy of the merchant in your hometown—treat customers as a neighbor, not as a consumer.

Bibliography

Bell, Chip R. *Customer Love: Attracting and Keeping Customers for Life* (Provo, UT: Executive Excellence Press, 2000).

Bell, Chip R. *Customers as Partners: Building Relationships that Last* (San Francisco: Berrett-Koehler, 1994).

Bell, Chip R., and Bilijack R. Bell. *Magnetic Service: Secrets for Creating Passionately Devoted Customers* (San Francisco: Berrett-Koehler, 2004).

Bell, Chip, and Oren Harari. *Beep Beep! Competing in the Age of the Road Runner* (New York: Warner Books, 2000).

Bell, Chip R., and John R. Patterson. "Command Presence: Animate and Engage People," *Leadership Excellence*, December 2005.

———. "Customer Intelligence through New Eyes," *Customer Relationship Management*, March 2004.

———. "Don't Skip Dessert," *Customer Relationship Management*, June 2004.

———. "New Rules for Mining Customer Intelligence," *Customer Relationship Management*, October 2003.

———. "Service Metrics: Using the Dashboard to Drive Customer Intelligence," *Customer Relationship Management*, December 2004.

Bell, Chip R., and Heather Shea. *Dance Lessons: Six Steps to Great Partnerships in Business and Life* (San Francisco: Berrett-Koehler, 1998).

Bell, Chip R., and Ron Zemke. *Managing Knock Your Socks Off Service*, second ed. (New York: AMACOM Books, 2007).

Berry, Leonard L. *Discovering the Soul of Service* (New York: The Free Press, 1999).

Bird, Anat. "ERM and the Bank's Culture," in *The Bank Executive's Guide to Enterprise Risk Management* (Washington, DC: American Bankers Association, 2006).

Blanchard, Kenneth, and Sheldon Bowles. *Raving Fans* (New York: William Morrow and Company, 1993).

Block, Peter. *Stewardship: Choosing Service Over Self Interest* (San Francisco: Berrett-Koehler, 1993).

Connellan, Thomas K. *Bringing Out the Best in Others: Three Keys for Business Leaders, Educators, Coaches and Parents* (Austin, TX: Bard Press, 2003).

Davis, Larry N. *Pioneering Organizations: The Convergence of Individualism, Leadership and Teamwork* (Provo, UT: Executive Excellence Publishing, 2000).

De Geus, Arie. *The Living Company* (Boston: Harvard Business School Press, 1999).

DePree, Max. *Leadership Is an Art* (New York: Doubleday, 1989).

Eikenberry, Kevin. *Remarkable Leadership: Unleashing Your Leadership Potential One Skill at a Time* (San Francisco: Jossey-Bass Publishing, 2007).

Ellis, John. "Strategy," *Fast Company*, October 2002.

Gitomer, Jeffrey. *Customer Satisfaction Is Worthless; Customer Loyalty Is Priceless* (Austin, TX: Bard Press, 1998).

Godin, Seth. *The Big Moo: Stop Trying to Be Perfect and Start Being Remarkable* (New York: Penguin Books, 2005).

———. *Purple Cow: Transform Your Business by Becoming Remarkable* (New York: Penguin Books, 2003).

Griffin, Jill. *Customer Loyalty: How to Earn It, How to Keep It* (New York: The Free Press, 1995).

Harrell, Keith. *Attitude Is Everything* (New York: HarperCollins Publishers, 2003).

Heil, Gary, Tom Parker, and Deborah C. Stephens. *One Size Fits One* (New York: John Wiley, 1997).

Insana, Ron. "Wendy's Knew from Start Story Was a Hoax," *USA Today*, June 6, 2005, page 3B.

Kaye, Beverly, and Sharon Jordan-Evans. *Love 'Em or Lose 'Em* (San Francisco: Berrett-Koehler, 1999).

Keiningham, Timothy, and Terry Vavra. *The Customer Delight Principle* (New York: McGraw-Hill, 2001).

Kouzes, James M., and Barry Z. Posner. *Leadership Challenge* (San Francisco: Jossey-Bass, 2002).

Levitt, Theodore. "After the Sale Is Over . . . ," *Harvard Business Review*, September–October, 1983.

Michelli, Joseph A. *The Starbucks Experience* (New York: McGraw-Hill, 2007).

Peppers, Don, and Martha Rogers. *The One to One Future: Building Relationships One Customer At a Time* (New York: Doubleday, 1993).

Pine, Joseph, and James Gilmore. *The Experience Economy* (Boston: Harvard Business School Press, 1999).

Ragas, Matthew, and Bolivar Bueno. *The Power of Cult Branding* (Roseville, CA: Prima Venture, 2002).

Reichheld, Frederick. *The Loyalty Effect* (Boston: Harvard Business School Press, 1996).

———. *Loyalty Rules* (Boston: Harvard Business School Press, 2001).

Rosen, Emanuel. *The Anatomy of Buzz* (New York: Doubleday, 2000).

Sanders, Betsy. *Fabled Service* (San Francisco: Jossey-Bass, 1995).

Sewell, Carl, and Paul B. Brown. *Customers For Life: How to Turn That One-Time Buyer into a Lifetime Customer* (New York: Doubleday, 1990).

Steinbeck, John, and Edward F. Ricketts. *Sea of Cortez: A Leisurely Journal of Travel and Research* (New York: Viking Press, 1941).

Taylor, William C. "Get Out of That Rut and Into the Shower," *New York Times*, August 13, 2006.

Tichy, Noel, and Stratford Sherman. *Control Your Destiny or Someone Else Will* (New York: Harper Business, 2001).

Travis, Daryl. *Emotional Branding* (Roseville, CA: Prima Venture, 2000).

Wiersema, Fred. *Customer Intimacy* (Santa Monica, CA: Knowledge Exchange, 1996).

———. *Customer Service: Extraordinary Results At Southwest Airlines, Charles Schwab, Lands' End, American Express, Staples and USAA* (New York: Harper Business, 1998).

Zemke, Ron, and Chip R. Bell. *Knock Your Socks Off Service Recovery* (New York: AMACOM Books, 2000).

———. *Service Magic: How to Amaze Your Customers* (Chicago: Dearborn Trade Publishing, 2003).

———. *Service Wisdom: Creating and Maintaining the Customer Service Edge* (Minneapolis: Lakewood Books, 1989).

Index

About the Authors

CHIP R. BELL is a senior partner with the Chip Bell Group and manages its office near Dallas, Texas. Prior to starting CBG in 1980, he was director of management and organization development for NCNB (now Bank of America). Dr. Bell holds graduate degrees from Vanderbilt University and George Washington University. He was a highly decorated infantry unit commander in Viet Nam with the elite 82nd Airborne. Bell is the author or coauthor of several bestselling books, including *Magnetic Service, Service Magic, Customers as Partners,* and *Managing Knock Your Socks Off Service.* His work has been featured on CNBC, CNN, and Bloomberg TV and in the *Wall Street Journal, Fortune, USA Today, Inc.* magazine, *Fast Company* magazine, and *BusinessWeek.* A renowned keynote speaker, he has served as consultant or trainer to such major organizations as CVS/Pharmacy, GE, Microsoft, Home Depot, Marriott, Infiniti, McDonald's, Ritz-Carlton Hotels, Harley-Davidson, Pfizer, Lockheed Martin, Kaiser Permanente, Merrill-Lynch, and Victoria's Secret.

JOHN R. PATTERSON is president of the CBG affiliate, Progressive Insights, headquartered in Atlanta, Georgia. He has more than twenty years of executive leadership experience in the hospitality, business services, and real estate industries and he holds a graduate degree in business from the Darden School at the University of Virginia. His consulting practice specializes in helping organizations around the world effectively manage complex culture change built around customer and employee loyalty. Prior to founding Progressive Insights, Patterson's work experience included positions with NationsBank (now Bank of America), Homestead Village, Inc., Guest Quarters Hotels, Post Inn Hotels, and Trammell Crow Residential. His consulting clients include McDonald's Corporation, Freeman, VIRTUA Health, Compass Bank, Kaiser Permanente, Southern California Edison, Banco Continental, Pegasus Solutions, Banco Popular, General Growth Properties, Cousins Properties, EDiS Corporation, Manheim Auto Auctions, Cannon Company, and The College Board. He is the author of numerous articles in professional journals.

The **CHIP BELL GROUP** is a confederation of highly experienced consultants who passionately pursue one core vision—to help clients become famous for the kind of service experiences that result in devoted customers. All members of this long-term alliance are independent consultants with their own consulting practices. They periodically work together as a high-performance team on selected consulting projects. All of the CBG consultants share these key values: making cutting-edge contributions both to the profession and to their clients; practicing the world-class service they encourage their clients to emulate; and working to impart on their clients the capacity and competence to be more successful. CBG also produces training and delivers programs for all levels of the organization from frontline employees to executive leadership. Visit the group's Web site at *www.loyaltycreator.com* for additional information about consulting, keynotes, and training.

Chip R. Bell
1307 West Main Street
Suite B-110
Gun Barrel, TX 75156
214/522-5777
chip@loyaltycreator.com

John R. Patterson
1266 West Paces Ferry Road
#570
Atlanta, GA 30327
404/350-1746
john@loyaltycreator.com